"An Oasis in My Valley of Baca!"

By
Charmaine Sha'ron Perry

McClure Publishing, Inc.

"An Oasis in My Valley of Baca!"

By
Charmaine Sha'ron Perry

Original Copyright © 2005
2nd Edition Copyright © 2021

Scripture quotations from Amplified, New International, King James and New King James Bibles

Amplified Bible (AMP) Copyright © 2015 by The Lockman Foundation, La Habra, CA 90631. All rights reserved.

New International Version (NIV) Holy Bible, New International Version®, NIV® Copyright © 1973, 1978, 1984, 2011 by Biblica, Inc.® Used by permission. All rights reserved worldwide.

Scriptures marked KJV are taken from the KING JAMES VERSION (KJV) King James Version, public domain.

Scripture from the New King James Version®. Copyright © 1982 by Thomas Nelson. Used by permission. All rights reserved.

All rights reserved. No part of this book may be reproduced in any form except for the inclusion of brief quotations in a review or article without written permission from the author or publisher.

Publication Date: January 1, 2021

ISBN: 978-1734759525
LCCN: 2020924012

McClure Publishing, Inc.
www.mcclurepublishing.com
800-659-4908

TABLE OF CONTENTS

INTRODUCTION

PREFACE

CHAPTER 1 21

"Meet Ms. M – Queen of Mid-Life Valley Changes – Part 1"

CHAPTER 2 25

"Meet Ms. M – Queen of Mid-Life Valley Changes – Part 2"

CHAPTER 3 31

Valley of Wars: Body, Mind, and Myths vs. Reality

   PART 1 – MS. M's BODY AND MIND's SHENANIGANS MYTHS

   PART 2 – MS. M'S BODY AND MIND'S RUDE AWAKENING REALITIES

CHAPTER 4 45

Valley of Mid-Life Makeover Embarrassment

CHAPTER 5 53

Caterpillar Valley of Wiggling in Frustration

CHAPTER 6 67

The Divorce and Separation Valley: Shame, Hurting, Hiding, and Healing

CHAPTER 7 83

A Well of Oasis in the Valley

CHAPTER 8 97

Out of Baca Valley, But Still Thirsty

CHAPTER 9 105

Fresh Rain in the Baca Valley

CHAPTER 10 119

Out of Valley Detox and Moving Forward to Rehab

CHAPTER 11 131

God's Love Did Not Let Me Die in Baca's Valley of Tears

BIOGRAPHY

This Book Is Lovingly Dedicated To:

THE FATHER, SON, HOLY SPIRIT, AND MY ANGELS: *My Creator, my Redeemer, and my Guardian, Ministering and Warring Angels on assignment to me from birth till I am called from earth to eternity:*

GILBERT SHA'RON AND BETTY LEE MCREYNOLDS PERRY: My earthly God-chosen foster parents who adopted me and gave me their last name. Their Godly principles, spiritual foundation, helped me become rooted, grounded, and the woman of God I am today.

ORABELL CLEMONS AND EUGENE "THE JUG" AMMONS: For however and whenever the situation between you two occurred, my DNA results have confirmed at least one of your love encounter(s) physically produced and created my earthly existence.

MY CHILDREN: All of you have made it worth the struggle of single parenting. All of you not only love the Lord, but are working in God's kingdom for His glory: *Sherree Patrice (Ny) Brown; Galon Vancleef Ford, Rhonda Danjele' (deceased) and Kevin D. Greene.*

GRANDCHILDREN, GREAT-GRAND PUPS, AND ALL FUTURE HUMAN HEIRS TO COME: The existence and presence of each one of you have not only brought me great joy. You made those life struggles with your parents even more worth it all: *Dorian, Paris, Devin, Marcus, Isaiah, Lola, Blake, and Londynn Faye; and my three grand-pups – Cero, Grace, and Love.*

SISTERS RAISED IN THE SAME HOUSE BY MOTHER PERRY: *Pat and Maria* – although we were always signifying and telling Mother Perry on each other, thanks for being great sisters and giving great memories of giggling until our sides hurt.

ALL MY NIECES, NEPHEWS, AND COUSINS (NATURAL AND SPIRITUAL) – Too many of you all to name, but know I love and cherish all of you.

MY SPIRITUAL MOTHER: Who keeps me undergirded in prayer and is quick to tell me: "You're gonna learn one day God doesn't need your help! Go somewhere, sit down, and let HIM be who HE is!" *Mother Dorothy Lewis.*

FOR STILL KEEPING ME AND THE CHILDREN AS REAL FAMILY ALL THESE YEARS: *Michael and Vanessa Ford (aka Mikk and Rudy);* There are no words to describe what your one gesture and verbal expression of love did for me at one of the lowest times of my life.

MY OFFICIAL GOD CHILDREN BY DIVINE APPOINTMENT: The **Hollister's** (*Dave, Nique, Sandra, Ricky, and Amanda*); The **Richardson's** (*Rudy, Damond and Ebony*); The **Williams'** (*Karen, Marcie, and Chris*); *Charles Patrick Gooch, Nathan Jones, Frankie Leon, Apostle Lamar, and Overseer Katrina Johnson; Jolanta Peterson, Audrey Faye and Eddie Brown, Tracy Smith; and all my other spiritual sons and daughters' mentees.*

MY GOD-ORDAINED SISTER-FRIEND LIFELINES: Although life circumstances pulled us miles apart physically, you never ceased to pray, intercede on my behalf, chastise, rebuke, warn, encourage, support and helped me maintain my sanity, dignity, and value in God's eyes during the worst and best times for over 50 plus years: *Dr. Pastor Linda A. Powell, and Elder Rita A. Richardson; Dr. Apostle Bernice A. Williams, and Apostle Pastor Joy Ann Jones.*

MY GOD-APPOINTED SISTERS AND BROTHERS FROM OTHER MOTHERS: My reminders all real kin is not always the same genetic blood type kin: *Jan Blake, Debbie Brooks-Jones, Peronia (P. C.) Candidate, Rochelle Carter, Lewis C. Clark, Jr., William (Billy) E. Fountain, Linda Gathings, Sherlicia Grizzard, Joella M. Johnson, Leigh Floyd Jones, Angela*

Lester, Eula M. Love, Mary and Troy Mahaffey, Diane and Jerry Pierson, Melanee V. Roper, Jackie M. Shaw, Lennie E. Sykes, Bobbie Shepherd, and Pamela J. Woods.

DAH POSSE: *Shhh! That's our secret! You all know who you are. Nobody else needs to know* – they might try and bogart their way in and mess things up. Love me some y'all!

MY LEWIS-CHAMPLIN ELEMENTARY SCHOOL POSSE: The very first elementary school homies (including those who have transitioned from this earth to eternity): *Johnny Anderson, Sr.* (deceased), *Annie Ruth Holmes-Walker, Pastor Joyce Jackson-Hall, Lenore Joiner* (deceased), *Vickie Moore-Scaife, Phillip S. Paige* and *Delores Rhyme-Humphries*: New friends are okay and nice, but there's NO friends like our first childhood friends.

ENGLEWOOD HIGH SCHOOL LUNCHROOM "HOLY GHOST TABLE": *Pastor Dr. Nathan L. Schaffer, Elder Maurice R. Johnson, Bishop Sonny Peecher, Evangelist Adrienne Nuchols-Hardy, Pastor David B. Fletcher, Thelma Coleman-Parks, Larnelle Douglas, William (Billy) Fountain, Alfred Jordan, Elizabeth Lomax, Rhostegz Lomax, Albert McCants, Linda D. Peecher, and Dorothy Robinson-Whitehead.* Every Monday, we spent our lunch time *"playing church and imitating our Pastors, Evangelists, Prophets, Choir Members, Deacons, and Church Mothers!"* Isn't it ironic how we **ALL** ended up being in some form of ministry? None of us had a clue our Lunchroom Holy Ghost Table was actually God-setting us **ALL** up for the ministries most of us are in today!

ALL MY CHILDHOOD ANTIOCH CHURCH BUDDIES: *Way too many of you to name! Thanks for creating tons of antics wonderful memories, lots of fun times, mischief, and indelible lifetime memories.*

ALL THE PASTORS, MENTORS AND LEADERS WHO TAUGHT AND LIVED BY PRECEPT AND EXAMPLE: *For positively impacting and pouring into my life which created, shaped, and molded me into the Woman I am today! And....*

LASTLY, BUT CERTAINLY NOT LEAST – RONALD GERALD FORD – MY EX-HUSBAND AND FATHER OF ALL OF MY CHILDREN: *Thank you from the depths of my soul. We shared four years of courtship, 19 years of marriage and raised three beautiful, God-fearing children. It was a very huge and bitter pill to swallow that day you told me with tears in your eyes how you knew I was hurting and divorcing me was one of the most difficult decisions you ever had to make. However, you told me what I needed to understand was that you didn't have a choice! You <u>had</u> to release me because God revealed how you were hindering me from becoming all He had called and ordained me to be. This book is only the tip of the iceberg result of <u>your</u> obedience to what I could not - nor wanted to - comprehend the depth of the conversation on that day when you said it. May God's peace, love, and blessings flow in your life for your obedience on that day!*

INTRODUCTION

Since 2005, I have been trying to revise this book. I kept getting interrupted by this thing called "LIFE!" It was only after God navigated me through various life challenges, twists and turns, the reasons slowly begin to unfold. As a matter of fact, it was quite simple—I had not cried in the Valley of Baca (a/k/a – the Valley of Weeping) enough to move forward with this project. The knowledge of who God really is in my life, had not completely been revealed. The depth of His love for me, even when I did not (and still sometimes do not) deserve it. HE knows what is best for me—including my beginning and my ending. Despite any and everything—He had NEVER left nor forsaken me.

As this book second edition has finally come into full fruition, I look forward with great anticipation and excitement to have approaching my 73rd birthday on April 22, 2021. I have so much to thank God for and to be thankful.

Over the past forty years of the seventy-two years, I have faced many life challenges – emotionally, physically, spiritually, and financially. I have been loved unexpectedly by those I never expected to be loved by. I have been rejected and had backs turned on me by those I thought truly loved me. I have been disappointed and overjoyed – just like you may have been. Yet, through it all, I always knew way down in my inner most being, God had some very unique plans in His mind for me. The thing is, He never sent me memoranda about it. I had to totally operate in blind faith.

It was in 2010, that my biggest life challenges came, and they came back-to-back. Not only did they make me cry, but were the hardest, deepest, and longest that opened my eyes to this fact: I had not experienced my own gut-wrenching, uncontrollable, Valley of Baca season yet.

The Valley of Baca is a season that everyone will experience at least once in their lifetime. This is a season in life that throws one into a forced isolation. It is a time that will make people – especially those professing to be Christians – question not only their faith in God, but their own sanity.

My Valley of Baca season came through the deaths of the 103-year-old woman who raised me from age 18 months as a foster child, and eventually adopted me. Six months later, my 35-year-old youngest daughter transitioned suddenly and unexpectedly. There are just NO words to describe and express the pain, sorrow, agony, disbelief, anger, and grief attached to their deaths, let alone the endless tears. I eventually learned that humanly, we never get over death, no matter when, where, or how it occurs. God does, however, truly wipe our tears away and help get us through it. After all, He is the expert on losing a loved one, especially His own Son who died for our sins. Jesus Christ!

While Mother Perry was blessed to be here on earth for 103 years, she often begged God to take her home with Him because she was in so much pain. Naturally, it was very hard for us as a family to see her once robust body shrink to bare bones and deterioration before our eyes. She had lived a full and exciting life to the hilt, and always stated she was more than ready to "Meet Her Maker." A few months prior to her transitioning, she gave me specific instructions on exactly how she wanted things carried out at her funeral. She told me whom she wanted to do what, and who NOT to do anything at her celebration.

> She said, "Chaaa-maine – I don't want them folks who didn't even speak to me, getting up lying about what good friends we were. This is what I want done and I expect you to carry it out like I told ya! If ya' don't do what I told ya, I'm gonna raise right up outta dah casket

and say – That ain't what I told you I wanted!"

I responded, "Momma, if you DO raise up out of your casket, trust me and know this – ain't nobody gonna be left in that sanctuary to hear you say it, and Taylor Funeral Home will be guaranteed at least 50 new customers!"

Guess who was not taking any chances, and did exactly what she wanted? My hand is up. Can you see it?

While yet trying to come to terms and work through Mother Perry's transition, six months later, I got a phone call at 11:40pm on May 17, 2010, that turned my entire world upside down. That night confirmed my life would never, ever be the same. It was a phone call NO PARENT wants to or should ever have to receive.

I was at home alone and preparing for bed. The phone call bearing news of my youngest daughter Rhonda's unexpected death was so traumatic, that instantly I sensed something in me had died too. I screamed "No, Lord! Please let this be a mistake. They cannot be talking about my baby!" I was devastated, in shock and crushed emotionally. The whole scenario was so unreal to me in the natural, I felt like a main character in a sci-fi movie. I moved in slow motion after I heard the doctor say my daughter had gone into cardiac arrest and get to the hospital as soon as possible (ASAP).

Before I could hang up the phone and get over the shock, my phone rang again, and the doctor said she did not make it and had passed-away after the third attempt to revive her. That last call came so fast, I was still sitting on the side of the bed from the first phone call. I immediately fell on the floor screaming and hollering at God. I started cussing, throwing everything I could get my hands-on while asking Him why would He do this in my life now AND why so close behind Mother Perry? Through all that madness of hurt and grief, I suddenly felt a warm sensation hovering over my head. Then I heard a small still voice whisper – *Is what you're doing going to bring her back? Get up wash your face, compose yourself, call her siblings, Godparents, and a few others. Wait for them to come over here and take you to the hospital. You don't have to go through this alone*! At that very moment, I knew it was the Spirit of the Lord who had intervened. I did as I was instructed and somehow managed to push through the thought *this cannot be real* fog. The situation may have been real, but I was not prepared, physically, emotionally, spiritually, and most of all financially!

Rhonda was not only my youngest child, but she was also, and more importantly, my personal prayer warrior. I felt I would be totally lost without her. Even long after her death, I cannot begin to count the number of times, I would pick up the phone to call and tell her about a dog I saw dressed up like a human then slam the phone down after realizing she is no longer physically on earth. Then, every scene of the phone call from her doctor replayed like it just happened, and I would start bawling like water running from a faucet all over again!

Oddly though, something happened while making her final life-end arrangements. Yes, reality began to sink in, and I was hurting badly. However, just before I prepared to go to the funeral home, out of nowhere, God's peace engulfed me like a blanket. A new burst of strength came out of nowhere. I relaxed, started breathing easier, calmed down emotionally, and made it through the funeral arrangement process, even with the financial challenges. God showed up and out, more than I could have ever imagined. The Holy Spirit intervened and let me know that: 1) God knew from her conception how long He had planned for her to be here on earth; 2) there was nothing I could do that would bring her back to this earth;

3) she loved the Lord with all her heart and soul; 4) she had been trying to prepare and warn me right after Mother Perry's passing, that she would be transitioning soon herself; 5) the last month of her life here on earth were by far the best times with her in her 35 years; and 6) she has already made it to the place we are living to die for!

These revelations helped support the very emotional and difficult task of finalizing her earthly journey. Please do not misunderstand. There were many times during those days, I moved in slow motion. All during the finalization process and long after everything was over, I still cried uncontrollably. Thank God for the loving support of my family, close friends, 'Dah Posse,' church family, neighbors, friends in and out of town, her former classmates, co-workers and all those whose lives she had touched, to help me, her siblings, and God Parents, get through the process.

My most significant experience of crying a long time, was due to the loss of one so young, precious, and dear to me. Life is not so nice sometimes, and its events will make us cry. Life will devastate us, make us feel lost, unloved, unworthy, heartbroken, hurt, in despair, disappointed, etc. to the point you cry so hard and deep, you want to curl up in a ball and just die from those gut-wrenching tears!

Many readers will identify with some of the scenarios I present. Many will relate even in the first few paragraphs in the Preface. If so, then this book is definitely for you. All readers should ensure your reading seatbelts are securely fastened, because you're in for a hilarious and real-life adventurous literary ride.

If you cannot relate to *anything* I share in this book, either you're too young, too sanctimonious, or flat out refuse to deal with your own fallibility and reality! Another reading audience would be those who feel no one understands their plight, or their situation is isolated. While no two lives are exactly alike, I am sure readers will find at least one experience in this book that they can relate to.

Anybody who knows me already will attest that although I am truly a called and chosen minister of the gospel, I keep it real and raw! As such, I will be sharing firsthand accounts of some of the challenges I personally encountered. I will candidly and honestly reveal my frustrations, disappointments, heartaches, damaged emotions (some of which went back to my childhood and I am STILL struggling with), and my overcoming victories and successes that came with midlife challenges. You will meet my unwanted life-guest whom I had to embrace and accept as a life phase friend, named Ms. M! Oh, trust me, Sweetcakes, she WILL appear at your door and boldly declare, she has a divine right and mandate to enter your realm! Keep living! She does not discriminate, either she will also appear at your door as a male species as well! She *will* appear and bring all her cousins with her. You will find out who they are as you continue to read this book!

Feel free to laugh, cry, whoop, kick, scream, cuss, give yourself and each other high-fives, holler "Yes, Lord! That's me." This book was penned first under the unction of the Holy Spirit, and secondly to help my sisters and brothers understand life's maturing process in general. As we mature physically, emotionally, and spiritually, trust me – there will be many days that all you can do is cry. Life is not always nice or fair, but obviously, God has a purpose for making us cry.

Sometimes, during those down times in life when all you can do is cry. Remember, you are obviously still here on earth for a purpose, and you have a divine mission to fulfill. Trust me – life itself will make you cry. I cried through Mid-Life, but I did not die! God's love would not let me!

There is an oasis of hope and joy to be found in the valley of Baca.

> *For His (God's) anger is but for a moment, His favor is for a lifetime (or in His favor is life). Weeping may endure for a night, but a shout of joy comes in the morning.*

(Psalm 30:5 - AMP)

On the serious side, I will be sharing life situations that made me cry such as separation/divorce, single parenting, my own questions to God about life changing moments, how life made me isolate myself to hide pain and embarrassment, and yet come to know and accept that God truly has everything in divine order. The problem is, most of the time when going through these life challenges, we cannot see it because we are busy fussing and crying.

Readers will discover for themselves, just like they will surely die, they will also surely cry. The good news is it will not be always and forever. There *is* a light up ahead towards the end of life's challenging crying tunnels, and it is *not* a freight train. It is God bringing us safely out of our crying season in the "Valley of Baca" and riding into the next phase of life in Him.

It is my prayer that my readers fully understand how much God really does love us and is there for us in whatever phase life has us in at those moments of tears. May the eyes of your understanding be enlightened, as you read and discover that life is a daily learn and grow process.

> *Blessed is the man whose strength is in thee; in whose heart are the ways of them. Who passing through the valley of Baca make it a well; the rain also filleth the pools!*

(Psalm 84:5-6 - KJV)

God says this to you on today, "Go ahead and cry all you want child of mine! I created tears and the tear ducts! I AM GOD! I will let you cry – but I refuse to let you whither up and die in the Valley of Baca! While these earthly life challenges make you cry, you are constantly on my mind! I think peace, not evil towards you to give you an expected end in me. Then you will call upon me, and go and pray to me, and I will hear you. You will seek me and find me when you search for me with your whole heart. I will be found by you and I will turn away your captivity (of unnecessary tears)."

> *For I know the plans I have for you, declares the Lord, plans to prosper you and not to harm you, plans to give you hope and a future.*

(Jeremiah 29:11 NIV)

PREFACE

Before I get into the heart of this book, for anyone who has a loved one battling mental illness, this subject presents a short preface regarding a very touchy, ignored, devastating, and refused to be talked about – especially among 'church folks' and those calling themselves Christians that subject is mental illness! I implore you, please heed the signs, and seek professional help and medication.

The reality is, I do not care how saved, sanctified, filled with the Holy Ghost, speaking in tongues, etc. – we ALL need earthly help as well as spiritual help. Jesus not only addressed those possessed by demons. He healed those oppressed and who had mental health issues. Oftentimes we are so spiritual, we are no earthly good. Luke was a licensed and practicing physician who traveled with Jesus and the twelve disciples. Jesus obviously never had an issue with doctors, yet a lot of you do. How many do you know are in eternity because they refused to seek professional help.

As it relates to my daughter mentioned in the introduction, there were several hidden factors that came to light during her many episodes. There is not enough room in this book to describe the devastation I have personally experienced during her episodes. There were more times than I care to remember of the times I woke in the middle of the night, and she was standing over me with a knife in her hand about to stab me.

I did not know of her mental disorder during those times. As such, I would give my daughter rent in the form of money orders to mail or give to the landlord. To my horror, I would come home and see the money orders torn to shreds or even burned to ashes in the kitchen sink, with no way to replace them. When I would confront her, she would start crying and say she did not remember doing it. That is when I knew I had to seek professional help for her before she killed me or herself. Accepting and acting on this harsh reality was the first step towards both of our recovery.

For many years, I gulped, swallowed, and took the blame in silence for people accusing me of not handling my finances properly, but was always sharp as a tack with the latest designs. They could not understand why I was always dressed to the nines, yet always seemed to be on the brink of – and sometimes was – being evicted. That was not the case at all, but pride would not let me tell the truth. As it related to being dressed to the nines, people were always blessing me with clothes and household goods. I hardly ever bought anything new, and if I did, it was usually on layaway.

These mental breakdown episodes manifested more when she stopped taking medication to balance her out mentally. One thing about mental disorder patients is that when the meds kick in and start working, the patient stops taking their medication because in the recesses of their minds, they truly believe they are totally healed and do not need medication anymore. Their reality capacity is such they do not know that it is because of the medication, that they present a sense of 'normality'.

I was Rhonda's main support and caretaker during "episodes and outbursts" resulting from her not taking her meds. I was also an eyewitness to the miracle working of God being a 'mind-regulator', healer and deliverer. Rhonda started battling mental illness at age 19. It was a very long, tedious and draining battle for not only for our family, but friends and church family.

Mental illness is nothing nice, and oh – but for the grace of God, we could all experience it. However, with the proper diagnosis, treatment, medication, and God's supernatural intervention, Rhonda began enjoying and living a wonderful and normal life at age 23. She finished Junior College and Medical Technology Assistant School with honors, was gainfully employed for over eight years, got, and maintained her own apartment, bought a car, and was in a relationship. To me and others, she was living proof of the miraculous healing power of God. Even more importantly than her overcoming a mental illness demon, she knew and walked in her divine earthly purpose, and loved God. Her life and love for God is what has caused my tears to be less frequent.

CHAPTER 1

"Meet Ms. M – Queen of Mid-Life Valley Changes – Part 1"

Around age 35, my body started acting really crazy and weird! I did not know what was happening to me on any level – physically, emotionally, nor spiritually. My life presented me with a totally different agenda than I had on my life's event pages. My outlook on life took a completely different perspective as news of my childhood acquaintances' sicknesses and deaths became more frequent. I became scared when I realized I was acting exactly like those 'old as dirt and twice as polluted' relatives and church mothers I used to laugh at. You know the ones like you have. The ones we always laughed about at our 'kiddy's table'. Yes, those ones we would be in hysterics about because we all thought they were nuts. When they got together, instead of focusing on cooking our food, we would see them running around in the kitchen shouting and thanking God – and it was not even Sunday. Yes, *those* female relatives! Now, we are the ones being laughed at.

Amid too many of my childhood buddies being critically ill and dying, I faced divorce after four years of courtship and 19 years of marriage and having to raise three children alone. These things made the little sane emotions and self-worth shatter like glass! How in God's name could I handle all these body changes, emotional experiences, divorce, single parenting, and financial challenges by myself? I felt I would have a nervous breakdown. I could not fathom any way it could possibly be done, and the mere thought of it made me cry almost every day.

I thought because I was a Christian, I would always continue to look and be age 25, agile and thin forever! Somewhere in the recesses of my unrealistic, finite mind, was also the unrealistic notion, that I would always be married to my high-school sweetheart and father of all my children until one of us died! After all, not only were we Christians, but we were ministers and in leadership! Divorce simply was not an option if we were both Christians, right? I cried even more at the thought that, if divorce just had to happen, why in the Hell did it have to happen now, amid all these life changes, physically and emotionally? Was not it enough trying to cope with not getting into a size five dress anymore? Why was I put in this position to deal with this stuff by myself? The strongest epoxy in the world could never put my seemingly broken life back together again – *or so I thought!* God eventually proved me wrong on this thought!

Do you know that by the grace of God, a few miracles suddenly occurred? Do you know I really did eventually start crying tears of joy, instead of weeping gut-wrenching tears of sadness and sorrow? It happened overnight – 'Poof!' my unpredictable teens and their far-out mindsets, were taller than me and making high school graduation and college plans. How and when did that happen? How did I miss their growth and age spurts? How did they go from being in pre-school to college attendees and pursuing life passions and career paths? When did they arrive at the point where they could create and develop their own agendas, rational and sane religious, political, common sense views?

An Oasis In My Valley of Baca

When did I stop pacing the floor because I was concerned where they were, if they were in trouble, in an accident or God-forbid, mugged and left for dead? When did I become fully aware my pre-teens were now adults and in positions to take care of themselves? When did I finally realize that God had brought me through the whole nightmare of being a single parent, body going through unexplainable changes, and I was not crying about these situations anymore? Mainly, when did they have the nerve to decide they felt I needed to become a Grandmother to *their* children? Yes, I cried a lot through these phases, but God's love refused to let me die over any of them! Instead of being in Baca's valley of seemingly unending tears, I spotted fresh living water spring forth from the well in it!

CHAPTER 2

"Meet Ms. M – Queen of Mid-Life Valley Changes – Part 2"

Hey! What's up with this? Who IS this unwelcome entity? The audacity of her to think I am giving her the red-carpet royal treatment. She must NOT be from this planet, because she obviously does not know we do not operate like this in our earthly realm. Let me tell you about her so you'll have a heads up when she starts manifesting. She goes by the name Ms. M, but her real name is Ms. Mid-Life. She just pops up out of the clear blue, unannounced and in full regalia. She is never on anyone's agenda to entertain, and neither is she ever welcomed to anyone's personal space. I was young, thinking I knew everything, and did not listen! Those matriarchs and patriarchs of old tried to warn me and give me a head's up that she is sneaky like that! She gives no warning at all, and no one is ever prepared for her. She is literally a "hot and cold mess!"

It did not take me long to see how Ms. M had no regard for anyone's feelings and cuts up whenever she feels like messing up someone's moment. She is rude, intrusive, obnoxious and has no manners. She boguards her way into people's lives unexpectedly like a surprise Drug Enforcement Agency house raid. I was duly warned how no one's life is ever the same after her arrival. All I know is, I am my own best witness how Ms. M changed my whole life completely! I have had to adjust my schedule to fit hers because of her brazenness!

Ms. M had affected me so deep, I started wondering if anyone could see her tell-tale signs on me. Was it obvious to everyone who saw me that Ms. M was easing her way into my life as a permanent fixture? Did the people I encountered see the outward manifestation I had been sucked into Ms. M's life phase spider's web of no return?

Neither is she nothing nice. She causes a whole lot of stuff that's **HER** fault. For example, soon after she showed up, do you know my doctor visits immediately went from every six months to every other month? Because of her, my cholesterol, estrogen, and blood pressure levels started being monitored more frequently, my body hurt in places I did not even know existed and throbbed like a toothache – and not sexually either! To add insult to injury, she started cramping and twisting my body until *she* decides to uncramp and untwist it, so I can stand up.

That's not all! Do you know Ms. M affected my life so badly, she made my eye prescription change three times in one year! I also had to get a bigger sized cosmetic bag! Why? Ms. M affected my bladder area so badly, I had to start carrying extra undies, panty liners AND sweet-smelling feminine wipes. The only embarrassing insult remaining was pricing adult diapers – just in case.

Even with these unexpected but necessary body changes, it seemed like life tables had drastically turned. There was the time I sought pearls of wisdom, life nuggets and information from senior citizens. Now, *I am* that senior citizen *giving* the pearls of wisdom, life nuggets and information to the younger generation. I also find that I keep repeating myself over again and getting embarrassed when people get quiet. The reason? When I asked why they are not saying anything, they tell me I told them that two or three times already!

Ms. M will have people saying, "I remember when" and "when I was growing up, we did not…." a whole lot, too! Not so funny now as I remember Granny Grady and Mother Perry going into a room and not remembering why. I am doing the same thing and dare anyone to laugh at me.

Ms. M will make you feel out of place trying to "hang" with the younger generation. Their fads are way too wild and crazy and vulgar for your heart. I have concluded that today's society obviously do not believe in wearing clothes! Body parts like belly buttons and those used to be private parts beneath it, leave nothing to the imagination. I was taught as a child and young lady, to reserve everything from our belly button on down for your spouse, or yourself if you don't have a spouse. These days I see more stuff below on public display than I want to. I do not want to look in the mirror at my own stuff, so I definitely am not trying to see anybody else's stuff on public display. Earrings are worn everywhere but ears, and tattoos in places everywhere imaginable and unimaginable. Some even have arrows pointing directly to the unseen, secret parts! Somebody please get my inhaler, cause it's too much!

A lot of people think I'm just too old fashioned and prudish. They can call it whatever they want to. I call it self-respect and dignity, good morals, and decency, all of which seems to be a thing of the past. I hear young *and* old people openly discussing things they did the night before – or that morning – with partners who are not their spouses, same sex, or orgies! What happened to the moral, ethics, and sanctity of marriage? If this world's morals have stooped so low it makes me cry, I shudder to think of what our Creator is thinking and feeling.

One day, I kept interrupting my spiritual children's conversations asking what certain phrases meant! They think I am cool because they come to me in confidence with some real heavy stuff and know they can trust me with their darkest secrets. I do not condemn them but give them case scenarios with positive and negative outcomes and let them draw their own conclusions and choices. More importantly, I put myself in a position of confidence and trust with their secrets and struggles. As such, they also know I am not going to run and tell their parents, spread their business, or submit it as a church bulletin or media screen announcement.

They love me so much, a few of them got together to help me 'step up on my lingo game' and bring me 'up to speed'. I asked them what stage they were getting ready to put me on? Of course, they had to explain to me that meant "fill me in on the details." These are a few phrases I learned:

"*Off Dah Chain*" = Really, really good – not somebody's gold charm fell off their bracelet.

"*My Bad*" = Oops! My mistake, not a bad kid.

"*My Boo*" = a special someone like a boyfriend or girlfriend – not trying to scare someone.

"*Road Dog*" = Someone who's always available to hang out at any given time – not a dog running up and down the road.

"*Turn it Up*" = having a good time with your friends, not turning up the volume.

"*Kickin' It*" = chilling out with a friend, not kicking somebody in their kneecaps.

"*Fixing to Get Lit*" = getting ready to party, hang out and drink – not starting a fire!

An Oasis In My Valley of Baca

I was too excited to be *"in dah mix"* and have more information to minister to young people on their own level without judging them. However, here comes the monkey wrench! My new crash course in the youngster's lingo had Ms. M's other dried up senior citizen biddies *"Player Hatin"* (getting jealous)! They could not understand why all the young people started flocking to me and not them! Duhh! Maybe it was because I have *never* forgotten I was their age once and how some *"keep it real"* women came to me in love and showed me the right way to do things. Let me be clear though – it started at home first! The older, seasoned women just reinforced what I already knew. The young people do not go to Player Haters because they have proven to be unapproachable, mean, judgmental, bitter, unloving, cantankerous and have forgotten they were young once! Let some of these self-righteous old biddies tell it, they came out their mother's womb preaching, quoting scriptures and talking in tongues!

That is a completely new book right there in itself, so enough time and energy has been wasted on them. Let us continue with some more of Ms. M's shenanigans. Can any of my mid-life readers relate to some of this? I talk to my children more since they have gotten grown, than I did when we all lived in the same house. Hallelujah, amen, and kudos for the invention of cell phones, text/messaging, three-way calling, Facetime, Zoom, and all other social media connections. These modern-day technologies have made it possible to connect at a mouse click or voice command. Through these media sources, everybody can connect with each other, from any part of the world and keep up with each other. These features have also enabled me to reconnect with high school and college mates, neighbors, church members and co-workers.

Although Ms. M was not welcome at first, I eventually became use to her intrusions. On the positive side, it was through her, I gained a new level of respect from my children, especially now that they have children of their own. Fault finding and criticism of old is replaced with love, support, appreciation and understanding. They see first-hand why I did some of the things when raising them. We disagree without being disagreeable, and have amazing discussions on current events, sports, moral issues, and religion.

Looks like my motherly, child-rearing pearls of wisdom fell on good ground and took root after all. What really makes me chuckle though, is when I see them do and say things to their children, they swore they would never do when they had children of their own.

My little eaglets grew into adulthood overnight, and life tables turned in my favor. They have embarked upon their own life journeys of adulthood. God has set me free to enjoy and flow freely with life. Now they have to find ME via cell phone, voicemail, text, and social media. The good news is, if I do not want to be found, I can program my phone to go directly to voicemail and it drives them bonkers!

I made it through, tears and all, but by the grace of God, they made it and they are all right. Yes, they may have slipped and missed it, but prayers covered them, and love kept them and brought them through – just like our parents' prayers and love brought us through.

Ms. M gained her a couple of points here but trust me – I am still watching her very closely! God's love still prevails through tears, even while raising our children AND Mid-Life Crisis – whether we are single parents or married!

CHAPTER 3

Valley of Wars: Body, Mind, and Myths vs. Reality

With the help of God, I was able to reach and pass the child rearing and divorce recovery life challenge miles. Like the substance and alcohol abusers, the first steps to my recovery was to accept and admit. I had very low esteem, felt afraid, lonely, abandoned, unworthy, guilty, and kept thinking everything was my fault. I felt if I had done this or that or would not have done this or that, everything would be honky-dory and different. I did not know at the time, what happened was God-ordained. It HAD to happen, mainly because it was NOT the person God had ordained for me to be with in the first place. However, God has given us wills and here are three of them: 1) Perfect; 2) Submissive and 3) Your Own Will! He loves us enough to allow us to make our own decisions and He honors those choices we made.

I soon realized I had to get it together because I had to raise my children alone. The second reality was that my body and Ms. M was showing evidence that my body, mind, and emotions were going through very serious and uncontrollable changes. However – for the life of me, I could not understand why my Body was cutting up big time! My Body started rebelling totally against everything my mind told it to do. If you can recognize or relate to some of these things. If you cannot or do not, you have not dealt with your own reality.

PART 1 – MS. M's BODY AND MIND's SHENANIGANS MYTHS

This list may upset some readers because it will force them to face the fact that they're getting older and do not want to face the reality of it! Well, there are a few alternatives, that you can choose from you know – nursing home, mental ward, homelessness, permanent residency in a hospital, and clergy standing over your remains quoting "Ashes to Ashes and Dust to Dust"! Get over yourself, go with your God-given flow of life and accept the life changes with grace, dignity, and honor.

Here we go:

1) You notice how young men suddenly start saying, "Yes, Ma'am,"

2) Young men insist you enter doors and get on buses first,

3) Young men in the grocery stores insist on helping you put groceries in the car for you and refuse to take your tips,

4) Your body does not move as fast as it once did, and when it does get to moving, it hurts,

5) You do mental flips and cartwheels and go into a ridiculous praise when you realize you woke up on this side of the earth,

6) You get confirmation you are not six feet under in a good-bye box and white cement sealed vault or when you recognize familiar surroundings,

7) Number six realization sends you into an automatic praise of thanking the Lord for waking you up to see another day,

8) When your Body wakes up, its bones throb like a toothache and pop like popcorn kernels as it attempts to get its bearings to just sit on the side of the bed,

9) Body slowly crawls out of bed and begins frantic search for eyeglasses and finds them under the covers, inside the book they were reading the night before, or worse – on top of body's head,

10) Body needs glasses to make sure it gets to necessary room for early morning ritual without bumping into furniture or wetting on self,

11) Body's eyes needs bifocals to read any type of printed material,

12) For those who wear contacts, Mind has to remind Body's hands not to rub sleep out of eyes to hard because contacts are in them,

13) Mind has to remind Body that contacts are disposable – not permanent! After two months of not taking contacts out, Body proves point by turning eyes vampire red and running water like a faucet – due to over-extended wear and not taking contacts out to clean,

14) Out of nowhere, the sewing needle's eye has shrunken, hands will not stop shaking long enough to thread needles and makes Body frustrated and exhausted from the effort,

15) Body suddenly craves health foods more than fast foods except for once a month when Body must make its presence known to favorite the neighborhood chicken shack and rib joint,

16) Body has become irresistibly drawn like a magnet to fresh fruits and vegetable sections of grocery stores,

17) Body's stomach now repels and quickly eliminates greasy, fast foods from top end, bottom end, and even both ends at the same time, and

18) If Body's feet are stood upon more than two hours, feet start aching and swelling. Feet are no longer comfortable in three to five inch heals with toes out, ankle straps. Body's feet obviously forgot one of its trademarks was sharp, jazzy, unique, and bling-blingy stiletto shoes! Now, Mind must constantly tell Body to always have flat shoes in large purse – especially on Sunday. Feet are now in a perpetual love affair with fully cushioned, orthopedic, thick soled one inch to one and half inch shoes. Wait a minute! Did not Body's mouth laugh uncontrollably when it's mother and grandmother wore those same type of "Old Lady Shoes" when we were kids?

To add further insult, Ms. M took it upon herself to start forming bunions and calluses on once-upon-a-time, pretty and small feet! Instead of wearing size six medium size shoes, Body's feet are struggling to get in size eight and a half wide, trying not to wear size ten. Pedicures have increased to keep calluses from getting too hard and sore. What Granny Grady said: "Chile, when your feet hurt, *err-thang* hurts" when I was growing up, has now become my reality!

After all the shenanigans and feet issues, Body decided to go ahead and seek Dr. Podiatrist's professional help regarding issues with feet. I kept telling Dr. Podiatrist to remove bunions and calluses immediately because I needed to recapture my feet prettiness. Dr. Podiatrist must have had a conversation with Ms. M before I came for consultation! Dr. Podiatrist made Body and spirit wilt in shame. He absolutely refused to remove unsightly bunions from Body's feet. When I asked why, Dr. Podiatrist said if bunions were not bothering or hurting me, then Body nor he needed to bother them! Then, he told me my ego, vanity and cosmetic desires were *NOT* a valid enough reason for a bunionectomy. Then, the unthinkable statement came out of Dr. Podiatrist's mouth. He emphatically stated: "Our Body's feet tend to get larger with age, along with Body weight gain." What the whaaaa? That meant Body could no longer fit into Cinderella shoes. Body's feet have turned into the stepsisters' sized feet, and Cinderella is now history. **SCORE? Ego: -1,000; Life: 10,000,000!**

Body and Mind purposed to follow orders of Dr. Podiatrist. Mind's emotions were wilted worse than a rotting head of lettuce. *Ms. Reality* – cousin of *Ms. M* – boldly declared, "These things come with life as we get older!" The good news was, to Body and Mind's surprise, feet found a whole lot of relief inside those larger sized, wider width shoes. Somebody pass Body the gallon of Epoxy, please! Why? Body and Mind's egos both need to be pasted back together again.

As fate would have it, all Body's other parts decided to participate in the *"New Lifetime of Aging"* benefit party hosted by Ms. M. We will now discuss the great Mall adventures with Ms. M. Heaven help Body, Mind, *and* the Mall, if Body's Grandchildren are with it. Body and Mind got smart! We do not go to a Mall—or anywhere else for that matter—without a specific game plan. Body tires out too quickly on these adventures. Body's heart palpitates and head throbs in uniform protest! Body screams to owner to hurry and get it out of Mall before it falls on Mall floor! Mind tries to steer Body to the parking lot in a hurry! Mind finally got smart and developed a strategic plan for future Mall adventures. It goes like this. Mind first decides if Body really needs to go to the Mall in first place. If answer is yes, Body's eyes searches Google and pulls up map of Mall it's planning to visit. Mind then decides what stores Body plans on going to and where said stores are located. After obtaining that

An Oasis In My Valley of Baca

information, Body prints out Mall map and circles all stores it plans to visit.

Body makes big red circle indicating all necessary rooms (a/k/a bathrooms) before leaving home. Then, Body goes to necessary room BEFORE leaving home. Once in Mall, Body goes around Mall structure in circular formation. Body goes to stores closest to entrance, finds Food Court to take a break, and makes sure necessary room is by Food Court. Body continues Mall journey on opposite side of Mall and exits out to parking lot. If Body decides it just must go to Upper Level in Mall, it finds escalator and follows the same pattern as lower level.

Body and Mind notice and determine Mall architects must really love their mothers and grandmothers. There are benches and rest areas available every three or four stores. Now that Body's Mall visit has ended, it is faced with the ultimate challenge. It cannot remember where it parked its vehicle. Thank God for remote FOB's that help locate vehicles. The downside to this is, Body's ears hear eight to ten other car remotes from other seniors looking for their vehicles, too!

Body does not always act very nice in public. Body has firsthand experience in knowing its bladder does not always display nice manners, follow proper etiquette and protocol in expelling its contents. Body's bladder really cuts up and expel things from its lower body when it decides on its own to cough or laugh too hard. Body's owner has learned the hard way to always keep extra undies and wipes in purse, just in case! Neither does Body now laugh at older, refined women at public bathroom sinks washing out underwear!

Ms. M has body shutting down and craving sleep between 8:30-9:00pm. It was only a few days ago that Body did not even leave the house until after 10:00pm. Body used to stay up until 4:00am, take a quick nap and get up fully refreshed at 7:00am, with no side effects. Now, Body needs every ounce of strength just to get key in front door after being out for 15 minutes. Then, once inside, Body must take 30 to 45 minutes senior citizen power naps. Unfortunately, what was meant for 30 to 45 minutes, ends up being two to three hours! Body tries to watch TV, but TV usually ends up watching Body. Body has finally determined real reason behind invention of cable TV. It was designed so mid-lifers and senior citizens would not be embarrassed and afraid when they wake up in front of the TV in the middle of the night. Meaning, when a movie or home shopping promotion is going on, when they wake up, they no longer think they're in the middle of a sci-fi movie or have died.

Were these shenanigans enough for Ms. M? No way! She painted Body's hair salt and pepper overnight, with more salt than pepper. Body went to bed one night with sandy brown hair and about four strands of gray hair. One morning, after Body's eyes looked in the mirror, and Body's hair looked like a combined salt and pepper shaker. The onset of Ms. M's paintbrush came so suddenly, Body's son thought owner forgot to rinse conditioner out of its hair.

Out of revenge, Body colored hair blonde to make salt part look frosted. Body got Ms. M good and showed her a thing or two! Unfortunately, Body's hair grew so fast, it was at the beauty supply every week trying to keep the gray covered. Body and Mind are still not convinced the beauty supply owner's SUV was not bought with Body's hair coloring purchases alone. Body was in the beauty supply store so often; it developed a first-name basis with owner and started getting 20% discounts every time it went there.

Another thing Ms. M did. She made Body start needing a lot more lotion, facials, and body oils to keep it smooth. Body's skin started resembling crocodile skin if it was not oiled and greased up every morning. Depending on how

Ms. M felt, she sometimes had Body oiling up ashy skin two-three times a day.

Body's once-upon-a-time complete set of natural pearly white teeth suddenly had to be capped, fitted for partials, and eventually replaced. Before dental reconstruction, Body's mouth stopped grinning as much as it once did. Body's mouth started to resemble broke-tooth comb! Instead of brushing teeth before going to bed, Ms. M has Body removing teeth out of mouth and placing them in a cup filled with denture cleaner. It took Mind and Body a while to remember they no longer had a full set of their own pearly white teeth. On many occasions, both entities were embarrassed to realize Body had been walking around all day, grinning like the Alice in Wonderland Cheshire cat, and dentures were still soaking in a cup at home!

Let us not forget how Ms. M takes it upon herself to blow Body up like a helium balloon! Body was at a total loss, because it eats much less now than it did 20 years ago. Body is so tired at the end of the day; it forgets to even eat and goes straight to bed. Body's metabolism stopped working in Body's favor. Body and Mind concluded that they would love themselves where they were, no matter how big or small they were. Happiness slowly creeped back in to Mind and Body when Body realized it still had breath in it. Mind was not happy about Body's weight gain but came to its senses and they both started celebrating life. At least, Body did not look like some other bodies it encountered. This Body did not look like a wrinkled prune. Its skin was still smooth and was told it looked younger than what it was. Mind informed Body right foundation garments are available to help camouflage its over-abundant places if need be!

We are nowhere near done with Ms. M. She even shows out with Body's Family Physician. Dr. Practitioner comes into play and adds more insult to Body! Dr. Practitioner had Body endure pure torture on a treadmill stress test. Poor

An Oasis In My Valley of Baca

Body had so much pressure in chest, it felt like cement blocks had dropped on it. In all honesty, Mind thought Body was having a heart attack. Nurse kept telling Body it only had to endure a few minutes more. To Body and Mind, however, it felt like two days more.

After treadmill test, Body felt like it needed several oxygen tanks to recover. Body's head was swimming, heart felt like it would explode, and knees started buckling from under its legs. Nurses tried to calm and reassure Body and Mind the worst part was over, and they had done fine. However, the pain in Body's chest was so intense, felt like it should be in cardiac ICU instead of treadmill room. Body and Mind both felt they had just finished their earthly course and was about to greet Jesus and all its loved ones on the other side.

When Dr. Practitioner told Body results, there was good news and bad news. Good news was Body had heart issue, but could be alleviated by proper care, medications, and light exercises. Bad news – Body had upper respiratory infection, mild hypertension, and pressure in chest was caused by a strain in chest muscles around heart from lifting heavy items. Boy, oh boy! Ms. M seemed to be having winning touchdowns and using my Body and Mind to score points. Thus far, she has such a lead, Mind stopped counting points.

After all of this, Dr. Practitioner felt it was his duty to admit Body for an overnight stay and order more tests right away. Mind nor Body was ready to hear that news. Mind asked Body if it would rather be inconvenienced for one night or end up on a gurney in the basement wearing a toe tag. Mind won! Next day, x-rays and tests revealed a thing called 'costochondritis'. In plain English, that means the muscle that connects chest ribs to the breastbone was inflamed. That's why Body felt like a ton of bricks was in its chest. Thank God, it was not an actual heart attack! Body was ordered on bedrest for two days, not participate in strenuous activities or lift anything heavy. No exercising of any kind until Dr. Practitioner released Body to do so.

Was Dr. Practitioner finished adding insults to Body's wounded ego? Nope! He went twelve steps further and prescribed diuretic medicine to run excess water out of Body and bring pressure down. This was way too much for Body and Mind to handle in one day. Dr. Practitioner prescribed lowest dose, but Dr. Practitioner obviously did not know Body was already going to the necessary room every half-hour. Now Body will be going every five to ten minutes. Where is Ms. M? She's getting ready to receive a beatdown!

Body and Mind put on its 'big girl undies' and dealt with it head-on. It was not nearly as hard to do as Body and Mind thought after all. Both entities are still here and doing okay 35+ years later. She gained a couple of points on this round, but not too many, though!

PART 2 – MS. M'S BODY AND MIND'S RUDE AWAKENING REALITIES!

While Ms. M was cutting up negatively in some areas, she did bring some positive and enjoyable changes during her visit. Her appearance manifested an unexplainable patience with Body's grandchildren, that was never experienced with Body's children. Body's role of "Granny" got sudden bursts of energy and had a ball with its grandchildren. Body and grandchildren, sang silly songs, played crazy games, and made funny faces at one another. These shenanigans obviously did not set well with Body's children! When Body's eyes met with its children's eyes, they saw expressions of disgust because Body was rolling around on the floor like a three-year-old. Body itself became more disgusted than children at how long it took to get Body off the floor. Ask Body and Mind if either of them cared. They will both tell you it's the most fun they have ever had!

An Oasis In My Valley of Baca

On a more serious note, Ms. M had Body and Mind's owner at a very unfamiliar and scare stage in life. Society calls the stage "Mid-Life Crisis" because everything becomes a crisis overnight because everything changed overnight! The sad reality is, many people going through this Mid-Life phase cannot, don't know how to, or do not want to deal with the pressure and feelings of discomfort it brings. Mid-Lifer's Bodies and Minds prefer to wave unrealistic "My life is okay" magical denial wands instead. This Body's owner knew for a fact, its mid-life concerns and changes were very real. Mind wanted to deal with issues head-on, but Body's mouth was afraid to mention mid-life changing concerns with anyone. Both were afraid of what people would think and say, or not understand Body and Mind's concerns.

Mind also remembered the time Body was around age eleven. Body's ears heard some women openly comparing notes about 'night-time visitors. Mind instantly thought all the women were cheating on their husbands, because all of them talked about men named the Itis and Tism Brothers climbing into bed with them the night before, waking them up out of their sleep, and even getting up with them that morning. Mind even recalled one woman saying these brothers were so bold, they did not even go home and were still around.

Even at Body's young innocent age of 11, Mind wondered how these women's husbands must have felt about other men sharing the same bed with their wives. Mind became embarrassed to even think these women did not care other people heard them all discuss these Itis and Tism brothers, too. Mind thought, these brothers must come from a very large family, because they seem to have visited a whole lot of bedrooms at the exact same time. The other thing Mind's brain thought was the Itis and Tism family obviously did not have manners nor good home training, either. Mind thought this because Mind's ears overheard one of the women say how hard it was to get them to leave, once they got there.

Side note: Body's Mind clearly remembered the many times it had to sleep in the bed with its Granny because relatives dropped by unexpectedly. Some of you readers may have some of them as well. They're the ones who pop up and say they were just "passing through" on their way somewhere and decided to "surprise the family and stopped by to say hello"! They surprised the family alright, because they ended up staying six months.

During Ms. M's stay, some clarity of this Body and Mind's mental state. It came as Mind recalled another of these women's discussion about their bodies experiencing alternating fanning and sweating sessions. The women went into very lengthy discussions regarding these 'episodes. Mind remembered them calling this adventure their own "camera bulb flash moments, and private summers and winters." The women said they never knew when their flashbulb would go off! They were too hot one moment and five minutes later, complaining how cold it was. Most of the women expressed surprise and could not understand that when those 'episodes' came, everyone got up and left out of the house! Well, now this helped Body know it was not alone in the camera flashbulb experiences!

Another area that explained it for this Body, was when Mind further remembered Mother Perry, Granny Grady and older Aunts always talking about late-night surprise bed partner visits, named the Itis and Tism brothers. Seems these brothers were so familiar with their Body they were all on a first name basis. In case any readers have not met this family yet, allow me to introduce them to you. Trust me, if you keep living, not only will they manifest, but they also will be when you least expect it! Their names are: Arth R. Itis, Burr Si Tis, Tendon It is, Cole It is, Bronch It is, and their first cousin

An Oasis In My Valley of Baca

Rheuma-Tism! Mind admonishes readers to remember their names well, for this page will not be your first or last introduction to them!

Please be ready! Members of this family are very shrewd. They sneak into bedrooms at night, immobilize and fix it so Bodies cannot move. Suddenly, Body wakes up one morning and realizes it's been invaded by some unknown and unidentifiable entity. Body experiences so much pain and agony, its mouth cannot even scream for help. Their invasive, secret late-night attack tells everyone about Body's experience through visible manifestations. Mind and Body's mouth are in constant warfare against overnight invasion. They begin to quote healing and deliverance scriptures and affirmations to rid themselves of the torture. Unfortunately, for Body and Mind, everyone they encounter knows they have had a few secret rendezvous affairs with Itis and Tism family members. Body and Mind also were horrified to learn this family consists of nothing but "playas and body violators!" They violate and unlawfully enter every human body they can. They're experts in playing with minds, will and emotions if the body and mind allow these heathens to do so.

Body and Mind were further appalled to not only learn the above, but they molest and sleep with men as well as women! Both sexes experience marked differences in their bodies. Victims of these aggressors makes its victims start walking slower and difficult to move as fast – or as often as they once did. Bodies feel like they are walking around 12 months pregnant with triplets! After the Itis and Tism family invasions, everyone's Body and Mind encounters know Body's secret. It has been lured into a love affair encounter of the "Itis-Tism" king. Then, it gets even more difficult to deal with. Out of nowhere, everyone who has been seduced and raped by them starts volunteering their own personal encounters of this family's intrusive behavior. It's worse than the local church's mid-week Prayer and Testimony services. Everyone in attendance feels no one can tell their testimony like they can tell it, about this family's painful and invasive shenanigans. Either they were delivered from them, wrestling with getting delivered from them, or just finding out about their need for deliverance from them.

Mind had to get in its digs by reminding Body of owner's disobedience to Mother Perry and Granny Grady when growing up. Body would be disobedient and refuse to cover head, chest and legs when going out in below zero freezing Midwest weather. Body felt it was too cute for wool hats, earmuffs, thermal underwear, heavy coats, scarves, boots and two pairs of gloves. Now, Mind teases Body because it must take meds for upper respiratory issues in the form of bronchitis – and avoid extremely cold weather as much as possible!

CHAPTER 4

Valley of Mid-Life Makeover Embarrassment

Body and Mind was slowing coming to grips because they knew these things were really part of the life maturing process. The message became clear they could not avoid this phase in life, nor resolve it on their own.

Body's mouth eventually got enough courage to express its concerns to a few associates around its age. Body's ears wanted to know if their bodies were having the same issues and concerns. Their answers were yes, but like this owner's body, was too afraid to mention it for the same reasons. Hallelujah! Body started jumping up and down in excitement, and mind was secretly thanking its Creator because it was proven its owner's Body was not an isolated case!

Body and associates' bodies and minds purposed to do something constructive to reclaim their dignity and self-worth. Everyone's minds and lips vowed to start eating properly, eliminate unwholesome foods, activities, and people. All bodies left the restaurant and met at the closest gym and enrolled. As fate would have it, the gym had just

An Oasis In My Valley of Baca

launched a new low-impact program for women over 35. Everyone was excited, recharged, determined and anxious and to begin the following Monday. This is where the real deal of reality sunk in for all.

The first aerobics warm-up session quickly negated our mind-set theories of "We still got it and can do this thang, honey" theory. Minds said, "Come on, Body, let's do 50 crunches and deep knee bends like you used to do back in the day!" Bodies told Minds they were crazy because it should know Body cannot do those things anymore. Minds kept insisting Body could until Body's mouth screamed at the top of its lungs to all the Bodies – "Oh, yeah? Not you cannot. *SURPRISE!!!*"

This life boxing ring match Minds were ahead of Mid-Life Bodies 2,000 to 0! Minds were still pumping Body's head it could do it, while Bodies were acting in direct contrast. Bodies sweated, gasped for air, and cried out in pain. Mid-Life Bodies also fell out on gym floor after third Stair Master attempt. Mind felt Body's heart was going to burst out of its chest even after Body's arms tried to bend down and touch toes. This Body's owner could not understand what was really happening! Body was not cooperating with its Mind, so Body lashed out in retaliation and protest!

No one's Minds could understand what was happening. Everyone felt confused. Minds were steadily trying to convince Body it was only trying to help. Body, in turn was rejecting and hurting all over. Mind had a hard time comprehending the issue. All it did was tell Body to bend down and touch toes. Mind was only trying to help coordinate limbs and other anatomy parts. Mind gave Body some consolation when it reminded Body at least stomach did not look like it was twelve months pregnant and could at least still see its toes without looking in a mirror to do it.

An Oasis In My Valley of Baca

Then – the real fight began! Body's eyes spotted about six "Let me be up in the front so everyone can see MY cute, young, perfectly shaped, human doll figure!" These *wenches* had the nerve to be hopping and jumping with ease and looked like human wind-up dolls. Body's head became dizzy just watching them. The human wind-up dolls made Body's Mind get very disgusted and frustrated. Mind thought "How dare these human wind-up dolls flaunt their shapely and distinguishable body parts? Mind thought Body was going to a gym. It did not know it was attending an early Monday morning fashion show! Who do these human wind-up dolls think they are? Why are they all sporting colorful leotards and body shapers, so they can display their perfect shapes?

Who told them to have their not-a-strand-out-of-place hair like that? How dare them to even have wrist band, headbands, and socks matching? Why in the hell are they in the gym anyway? What fat did they have to rid themselves of life we Mid-Lifers do?

Mind and Body's experience became more frustrating as our "personal gym trainer" ignored all the Mid-Lifer's pleas for help with the gym exercise equipment. He was too busy knocking us down to get to the super-thin, human wind-up dolls. Maybe it was because the Mid-Lifers were not dressed and sexy and raunchy as the human wind-up dolls. If our bodies tried to dress like the human wind-up dolls, they would've looked like decorated circus elephants in ballerina tutus. Another factor was, we Mid-Lifers didn't have the time nor the energy to try and be dressing sexy for aerobic classes. Most of us were only concerned about Body and Minds mission to recapture lost size three to seven petite dress sizes. Our bodies gym attire consisted of oversized T-Shirts to hide Mid-Life bulges, and jogging pants with elastic waistbands, so if Body's stomach expanded, it wouldn't hurt. Body was NOT on a secret mission to impress and catch. The only thing Body was trying to catch at that moment, was its breath!

The Human dolls' anatomy didn't jiggle and resemble holiday Jell-O molds when they did aerobics, either! When the Mid-Lifer group tried Jumping Jack exercises, there was so much floor shaking going on, the rest of the aerobics class ran for cover. They thought another California earthquake had erupted.

Well, Body's mouth finally confessed its issues. Body and Mind was jealous of the human wind-up dolls energy and stamina. It didn't help their petite shapely bodies were a rude awakening and reminder of how us Mid-Lifers used to look and do. Body closed its eyes and told Mind to only think positively about those human wind-up dolls energy levels. Body closed its eyes, hung its head in shame and secretly asked its Creator to forgive Mind and Hearts negative thoughts and feelings.

However, when Body's eyes opened from asking forgiveness, they widened in horror! Body was seeing reflection of itself in a three-way mirror. Body's eyes saw its backside had gotten so wide; all three mirrors were taken up with it! Three-way mirror also showed thighs and hips full of dots, dimples, and craters, they could have easily been mistaken for a truck filled with English Muffins with a "CAUTION – WIDE LOAD" sign across the back of it. Body and Mind emotions felt more withered than a head of lettuce. They felt all the steam presses in China would never be able to smooth all those wrinkles on Body again!

As you readers have probably figured out by now, Body just was not responding favorably to the aerobics adventure, like Mind thought it should. Body was strained, tired, sore, and felt like it had been in a ring with all the top boxing champions across the nation. Body was desperately trying to get those deep knee-bend pains out of its kneecaps. Body and

An Oasis In My Valley of Baca

Mind didn't know the aerobics instructors were on the verge of calling 911 because all the Mid-Lifers were sprawled across the gym floor like anatomy class cadavers. We were all crying tears of disappointment and pain. We all felt our Bodies and Minds could never recover from the shame and embarrassment of this experience.

One of our associates was honest enough to confess out loud for all the Mid-Lifers. She admitted how when she was young like them, she was petite, and moved around just like the human wind-up dolls were doing now. She added, time really does bring about a change, and she'd love to see them in 20 years. They will have moved to the spot we Mid-Lifers are sitting and watching. She further reminded us that we had accomplished our mission of agreement. We had come to the gym and gave it our best shot.

We could achieve our goals; we would just have to take a different mind-set and approach. The key factor was – we did it! We came there to better ourselves, get our bodies in shape and eat sensibly. We just must remember we did not gain weight overnight, and it will not come off overnight, either. However, if we remain consistent and committed, it will come off and everybody will see the results of our hard work paying off. We all agreed, jumped up and started dancing to the exercise music – sore bodies and all. Our new outlook made a huge difference. In fact, we ended up having so much fun, the aerobics instructor almost had to put us out!

Body and Mind successfully made it through that aerobics class with still a little dignity left. It was a positive, gigantic step of accomplishment for Body and Mind. They felt like they had moved the Rock of Gibraltar. All the Mid-Lifer Posse's spirits felt renewed, had new determinations, and positive attitudes, which unfortunately only lasted about fifteen minutes.

An Oasis In My Valley of Baca

This owner's Body and Mind could only speak for itself. This Body was very sore and still wrestled with a wounded ego on the way home. Body's eyes gazed upon many women who had apparently crossed their own bridges of Mid-Life challenges unsuccessfully. Body's Mind felt the reality of Ms. M.'s appearance was too traumatic for them. Some women looked like menopausal teenagers in the way they were dressed.

To make matters even worse, Body also encountered quite a few female acquaintances. They proudly introduced Body to their "boyfriends" who looked young enough and acted more like their sons and grandsons. One even had the unmitigated gall to boldly declare "the Lord sent him to rescue her, and they were on the 'way to the bank' to pay him for cleaning out her garage!" Mind wondered which garage, the car garage, or her physical garage. The other young man held his head down like he was embarrassed at his "boyfriend" title. The way she was dressed, I would have been too! **All** I could do was shake my head in disbelief. These two were female cougars in full manifestation.

Far be it from Body's mouth to shatter the cougars rose-colored glasses and cataracts – that is right cataracts, not contacts. A cataract is a film that covers up the eye lens, so everything is blurred. Glasses bring clarity to what is blurred. Cataract removal requires professional surgical skills. So, as it is in the natural, so it is in the spirit. We need professional skills to be healed. One thing I did know for sure, Body went home after the close encounters of the Mid-Life cougar kind and made a lifetime promise to its Creator:

Body and Mind solemnly promise to God from this day forward, on good days and bad days, to seek Godly wisdom and knowledge diligently and wholeheartedly through Body and Mind's aging process, so neither

An Oasis In My Valley of Baca

embarrass themselves, their loved ones, friends, neighbors, and church members by looking like certified menopausal teenaged idiots!

CHAPTER 5

Caterpillar Valley of Wiggling in Frustration

The previous three chapters were designed to help readers laugh about the realities of life through physical, emotional, and spiritual challenges. The next chapters will deal with crying through divorce, self-worth issues, confessing the need for help, getting through everything life was hurling at me, personal struggles of letting go, forgiving and moving on towards God's divine purpose for MY own life – not anyone else's.

There was so much happening from these challenges all at once, I felt like I was in the Wizard of Oz tornado. I did not understand any of it, and felt I was being punished for the 'sins of my fathers, all the way back to the ninth and tenth generations. It was so bad, I constantly cried, because I never knew what curve ball life would strike me out with next. I kept wondering and asking God how much more did I or could I take. My comfort zone was upheaved by Ms. M's arrival. She left me feeling confused, frazzled, scared, and isolated about the impending divorce status, my self-worth, emotional stability, physical unexplainable body changes and mood swings, and even my spirituality.

Way deep within; however, although I knew I was embarking upon some new kind of threshold, but it wasn't necessarily a crisis as the world knows it. As I gave serious thought to this phase of life change, I came up with a whole lot of questions to myself and to God.

I first wanted to know when this whole mid-life thing started for me. I felt I needed to go back into the recesses of my mind and try to determine if I had missed some valuable clues regarding the upcoming changes. My second question was WHY did it start and if this was a normal life process and thing women went through, or was I singled out to carry this challenge alone. God has been a real vital part of my life since I accepted Christ at age eight years old. Therefore, I not only could not understand why, I felt the way I felt emotionally, but that it was wrong to have these types of feelings at all since I loved God so much.

If God and I had such a great love relationship going, why couldn't I rid myself of these feelings of inadequacies and anxieties. I was taught by the best and learned how to cast all my cares upon Him, but there was no relief for me emotionally, physical, or spiritually. Why did I have these overwhelming visions of me looking like a squirming autumn caterpillar escaping the childhood prank of being set on fire in a pile of leaves?

These feelings and emotions surely did not feel very 'spiritual' and were totally out of whack from the way I had been raised and taught. There was a constant wriggling of my emotions and spirituality struggling to get out of an emotional autumn leaf pile. Rather than escaping out of the pile though, it felt not only like I was in the middle of the burning leaves pile, but also burning like coal in a winter fireplace.

In fact, the life alteration was so bad for me during that time, I was crying uncontrollably so much I even thought about admitting myself to a psych ward for in-house evaluation. My head hurt and the inside of it felt like it was going to literally explode in my head. Nothing made any sense to me at all at that time.

The only alternative for me during that time was to discreetly ask my Primary Care Physician for the on-call psychiatrist. The only reason I did not was because of my ministerial status, I was afraid there would be a health professional I knew who attended my church, working on that psych unit. It made me fearful and concerned that it would get back to my church. I surely did not want the hospital room number to be associated with a psych floor. All I knew was this – I needed answers and I needed them quick before I completely lost my mind.

The other thing that had me out of sorts was when I started thinking about all my childhood friends and classmates. I began to wonder where they were and what were they doing now? Were they happy and content, or going through the same or worse changes as me? If I saw them, would they look the same, better, or older than our grandparents? Would I still look young, better, or older than dirt? Were they like me, although everything was not peaches-and-cream, glad to still be on this side of the earth and not under it.

In my mind, I began to try and match faces of those I went to high school and college with and remember them. I still had my high school yearbooks at that time and tried to envision how they might look now. More questions! Are the once petite pom-pom and cheerleader squad babes now shopping in plus-size shops like me? Did the tables turn so now the plus-sized bubble-butt girls the sports teams laughed at, now are the ones sliding into sizes three, five, seven and nine sizes in a twist of fate?

Did any of my classmates achieve their dreams of successful careers, or were too many of them caught in a once-a-month disability and welfare check system? How about those buff, muscular and handsome star athletes? What are they doing these days? Were they now toothless, bald, pot-bellied alcoholics, crackheads, gangbangers, or drug dealers? How many of my male classmates were on the corners in wheelchairs with no legs, with tin cups due to being injury casualties of wars, homelessness, job loss and insanity due to shell shock and too vivid memories of their buddies exploding in front of them like fireworks displays? What potential millionaire status bound classmates were now homeless? How many were permanent mental patients on psych wards?

How many scholarly male classmates are spending the rest of their earthly days in jail or are in their eternal homes because of being with the wrong crowd or in the wrong place at the wrong time doing the wrong thing? What about those bullies and gangbangers that had the students and faculty afraid to cross them? Are they now using that same toughness and tenacity to preach the Gospel?

I was and am very pleasantly surprised at those latter ones who are in ministry that I have gotten reports about. The other good news is what I hear about those who were believers in high school still being on fire for God. There are quite a few who are Pastors, Apostles, Elders, Evangelists, Prophets, etc.

My questions continued during this reflection season. Which classmates had lost their dignity and self-worth due to drug overdoses, alcoholism, wrong or ungodly relationships? The most challenging and frightening thought was – how many of my high school and college classmates are even still alive?

Quite a few have died over the years, and my circle of those that yet remain was getting smaller and smaller. Some classmates died of serious illnesses, drug overdoses, accidents, murder and even suicide. However, the scariest reports of deaths were those five classmates I knew personally who sat down in a chair, stretched across their beds 'just to rest', or who went to bed the night before and woke up in eternity. Talk about reality checkpoints!

How could this possibly be? We were at the age of pre-senior citizenship – not actual seniors yet. Weren't we supposed to have at least a good 40 plus more years left here on earth? Why were so many my age, leaving earth? It hit just a little too close to home for me and made Ms. M.'s appearance start to lose those few points she had gained. I felt I had missed something, and wondered if I would ever be able to recapture time lost and rectify my wrong life choices before I left earth?

It seemed the more I sought answers, the deeper into depression the questions sent me. No one seemed to have answers, hear my cries of concerns, or even care. They were too busy dealing with their own issues, feelings, and insecurities. I became very frustrated. I did not know was I just closing out a normal life phase and being thrust into a brand new one. No one told me it was a normal process of life, and everything would positively work out. All I needed to do was, sit back, relax, buckle my seatbelt, put my shades on, grab my lemonade cup and sip from it while riding. I did not even have to drive. All I had to do was trust the driver to get me where I needed to be and enjoy the scenery along the route.

All the above was AFTER the fact, not during it. At that time, I did what I was supposed to do spiritually. I spoke positive words, tried not to look at circumstances in the natural, walk by faith – not by sight, yaddah-dattah-whoo-whoo! In reality, I was so out of joint emotionally, I could not get a good crawl in, let alone walk by faith. How and why should this be happening to me? The more I rebuked Satan, speaking the Word over the situation and myself, and told him to "Loose his hold," the tighter his grip seemed to become, and the more he manifested himself.

My finite mind led me to believe perhaps the negative power of my tongue had gotten me into this mess. Therefore, I started confessing positive things over myself and situations. Problem was, nobody told me I needed to KEEP confessing until it manifested into reality. It was not until much later in life I was taught seeds do not grow as soon as they're planted. It takes time for seeds to grow, and the soil must be watered to reap a harvest. Neither do all seeds have the same growth rate. Different seeds produce different harvests at different seasons.

If those around me knew what was happening to me on the inside during that phase in my life, they would be shocked. Especially the younger people I was associate with through ministry. They always commended me on how strong I was spiritually and emotionally. To them, I never allowed Satan nor life circumstances, to defeat me. They were wrongfully convinced I was invincible and expected me to be strong. I was the one they came to for help in keeping them on the straight and narrow paths. They had no clue I was hanging on to life by a sewing thread myself. No one was helping keep ME together. I had issues, was suffering in silence, and needed someone to come to MY rescue.

What would my church family think if they knew I had these kind of feelings and insecurities? I had not been taught yet to 'keep it real'. I was taught to not let anybody know I was hurting, had problems and insecurities. I was raised and led to believe I should grin and bear it, not express myself, and tell everybody the lie that I was just fine! In other words, the Strongman named "Lying Spirit" had full access and control.

An Oasis In My Valley of Baca

I had to continue in a La-La land of the great façade. The only thing missing from the scenario was a pill box hat, white gloves, a patent leather purse with matching pumps and a lacy white hanky. We could not dare let anyone break the glass ceiling of that facetious mold on that image! Nobody needed to know I had feelings and hurt just like everyone else. After all, I was a minister! Yeah – right! People forget ministers are human beings!

In reality, I was about to explode like a July fourth firecracker. I could not help anybody because I needed help myself. Behind closed doors, I was crying and hurting like those who came hurting and crying to me for prayer and guidance. To the 'elite Christians' it was out of order to disclose that we were not mini-gods and goddesses. We could be 'dethroned' from leadership positions if "WE" were subject to feelings, wrong decisions, and not have it all together in every area of our lives. It was unthinkable to reveal the great, deep, dark, realistic secret that we are 100%, bonafide, living human beings!

I asked God where He was at, and where was MY encouragement? I reminded Him that He said He would never leave me nor forsake me, yet I felt abandoned. Why was there such an upheaval that left an emotional hurricane affect? I was so messed up emotionally and spiritually, the thought of trying to encourage myself in the Lord, never came to me. I also told Him I thought His answers were *always* yes and amen! His response was my teachers forgot to tell me delay did not mean denial. Neither did it mean He didn't hear me, because He IS a promise KEEPER – not a promise BREAKER! I had to learn to be patient, stand, rejoice, thank, and praise Him for the manifestation in His timing and WAIT!

That was the revelation which finally made me start looking at my life from a different perspective. Ms. M. was not only changing me, but my entire life and surroundings, all of which I could NOT control. One of the first things I realized was, I was not the first nor only woman to go through this phase of life. It was just that no one was verbalizing it on the level I was. It seemed most women my age were looking through rose-colored glasses and saying, "All is okay in my world." The unfortunate for them, we saw the real deal in their behavior and thought they were two french fries short of a hamburger meal order. That was not my testimony!

I needed to talk to someone who first, would not think I had lost my mind completely. They had to also have already been there, gone through it successfully, and still alive (and willing) to talk about it. It was Mother Perry and a few other seasoned women of wisdom who came to my rescue.

One of them was a close friend who is not only an ordained minister, but a licensed and practicing Clinical Psychologist/Counselor. She had over 30 years in psychiatric nursing as well. She gave me some sample behavior patterns displayed by some Christians and church females who were on the psych unit. Some readers may recognize themselves. It's okay, because if you do, then there is also doable solutions, so you do not become a psych patient! That is one of the purposes this book is for – heal, set free, deliver, and make whole.

My psych nurse friend gave me a few of the typical "Candidate for Psych Unit" traits for church females' symptoms. She began the symptom list with this: Many of the church attending females in leadership positions were between the ages of 40 to 75. These women had been functioning in the same leadership positions or supporting their prominent husband's in leadership. They had done things the same way for so long, they did not realize life had changed THEM with time. In their minds, they still thought they were in their 20's and 30's. These same women were

An Oasis In My Valley of Baca

like those discussed previously. They were taught like me, not to show emotions or emotional pain.

They were also led to believe showing any sign of reality/realism was a sign of weakness and exposing the family business. To do so would reveal their human side, and their "Goddess" and infallibility façades would be over for good. This mindset in turn, created a great façade. Because of this façade, the character they portrayed became who they thought they really were.

The other piece to this is, many of these women – and their husbands, fathers, grandfathers, etc., held highly visible and esteemed positions in churches. However, the reality was this. In the confines of their own homes, behind closed doors (and sometimes even openly), these same high profiled, socially respected, leadership husbands were alcoholics, substance abusers, refused to pay bills, homo/bi-sexual, womanizers, pedophiles, gamblers, and wife-beaters.

These women kept up the façade by going out of their way trying to prove and convince everyone how everything was okay and how "happy" they were. What they did not know was, their real pain, unexplained bruises, bitterness, mental torment, and loneliness were very visible on their faces – and sometimes their bodies. My psychologist sister added, the main reason these women spent every available opportunity to be at church all the time was because their life at home was a living hell of mental/physical torture, emotional and physical abuse.

Before breaking down emotionally, these women busied themselves in various 24-7 social activities. It seemed that social participation gave them accolades not received at home. Self-worth and dignity for them came through heading auxiliaries, clubs, and other seemingly productive activities. When reality did set in, they ended up as patients on the psych ward.

Their psychiatric diagnosis: Mental battle fatigue from trying to be something they really were not – "An invincible Super Goddess!" They tried to be everything to everybody. For them, reality was non-existent. They forgot – or never learned – who THEY were! When reality did set in, it was too much for these women's emotions and bodies to handle. The women literally lost it and ended up being psych patient.

Because of denial, these women's bodies and minds entered to deterioration and stress-related conditions. Their mental faculties and bodies became worn and shut down from YEARS of hatred, emotional/physical abuse, years of pretense and inward bitterness.

Hold up gym shoes and socks! The revelation of these descriptions of symptoms and diagnoses hit a little too close to home for me. I was so involved in church activities at that time, I could hardly keep my house clean. I was always going to some meeting or program. I found out God was NOT pleased! While these "works and functions" did wonders for my ego and boosted my morale, it did little for my husband and children's needs.

My friend's synopsis helped me to see I needed to relinquish some activities, get things in proper Godly perspective, and concentrate on what God required to do. My house needed to be set in order with a quickness! God established the family before He did the church. It was time for some re-organizing, discipline and putting into practice the word **NO**!! Thank God I woke up and smelled the coffee before the coffee pot blew up in my face. I refuse to be issued a psych ward referral!

She concluded by saying if more women dealt with reality and their feelings like I am doing, it would help avoid being on a psych unit. This conversation made me

An Oasis In My Valley of Baca

determined more than ever to not ever be an initial nor recurring psychiatric statistic. My friend really helped me understand Ms. M. was a normal life process. God made us spirit first, then women of God, wives, mothers, sisters, evangelists, etc. God did not create us to be everything to everybody – that's HIS job. Our strength comes in being strong in the Lord, and in the power of HIS might! We can only drive one vehicle at a time. Find your lane and stay in it! Keep your eyes focused on your own lane and stay in it.

Another nugget of freedom regarding Ms. M.'s arrival. Please check yourself in the reality department. All of our life experiences will NOT be mountain top and laa-laa-ville ones. To think it even remotely is, makes us prime candidates for the psych unit. There is just no such animal living or dead. If we are always on the mountain top and never have a valley experience, how can we ever appreciate the mountain top experience? We cannot! There can never be a testimony about something we have never been tested in or been brought through.

To be whole, we must face our problems and issues head on and stop pretending everything is okay when it is not. Be real! Tell God you realize there is a problem, and you need to know how to make it right. Let me warn you, though. Brace yourself before you ask Him. He may tell you to do things unpleasant to your flesh and mind. It hurts emotionally, spiritually, and sometimes even physically to become whole if it's done correctly. God will first expose and shatter those hidden things in you. For the super-saints, the Holy Spirit may reveal you are full of pride, arrogance, and tradition. He may tell you to miss a few church meetings and hang out with your husband and children (I go into more depth about this in another chapter).

Time for the Mid-Lifers (and some senior citizens also) to burn their Super-Saint Goddess façade to ashes, reveal what is really going on to someone you can trust and openly ask for help. Once it's out in the open, the devil cannot hold it over you, nor torment you about it anymore. Here is a real TKO for you: As you get real with yourself and God, it may be revealed that you have been serving in a leadership capacity all those years, and never accepted Christ in your life!

It's not a sin to seek professional counseling. Luke was a physician who travelled with Jesus and the disciples, so Jesus nor God obviously did not have a problem with doctors. A whole lot of folks in the church need it. They are trained professionals who can walk you through processing your emotions, get to the root causes of negative behaviors and emotions. A bonafide Christian Psychologist, Psychiatrist and Counselor is one of the best allies a child of God can have besides Jesus. They take an oath to never discuss what is revealed to others. The main thing is, they are trained to not only deal with emotions, but the spirit man as well.

We must remain balanced. Ask God if you do not believe me. It's really all right with Him to have fun if it's decent and in order. Some church folks are so spiritual, they believe it's a sin to laugh. If God Himself laughs, what's their problem, then? God really does have a sense of humor. If you do not think so, look in the mirror!

Our female ancestors obviously went through mid-life before us and made it through all right, didn't they? They surely did! After all these revelations, I stopped writhing like a caterpillar in an autumn burning leaves pile. With my newfound knowledge, I hosted an imaginary caterpillar burning, fire extinguishing party. I refused to remain trapped in the clutches of uncertainty, anxiety, being an emotional wreck, getting on everybody's nerves and having pity parties. I had some life issues to face head on. Open the escape hatch door, Sweetcakes! I am no longer wriggling like a frustrated caterpillar in frustration and hot ashes. My

An Oasis In My Valley of Baca

tears have not only put the flames out but have evolved me into the next phase enough for me to fly out. *See ya!*

CHAPTER 6

The Divorce and Separation Valley: Shame, Hurting, Hiding, and Healing

As stated in an earlier chapter, my marriage crumbled around the same time Ms. M decided to show up. This chapter is to describe the deep emotional effects, self-realization, learning how to confidently ride on the winds of God's life changes, and help someone who may currently be experiencing the same situation.

A lot of people who knew and saw us, thought we were an ideal couple. To the outside world, we had it going on like Granny Grady's pot of neckbones. We had the typical storyline: Met in high school, dated almost four years, attended the same church, eventually married, and had children. There were the usual challenges and problems most married couples experience, so we were not unique in that regard. However, somehow God always managed to bring us through. Therefore, I just knew all down in my "shun-doe," this was another phase we were experiencing, and we would be all right. After all, we were Christians, God-fearing, and attended church regularly.

I was under the false fairytale illusion we would be together forever until Jesus returned. I even envisioned us sitting on a porch at a ripe old age, rocking into oblivion, surrounded by a brood of Grandchildren, Great-Grandchildren and even Great-Great Grandchildren. I was so unrealistic, I even felt if the rapture came, we would be caught up to see Jesus together! I know, pitiful isn't it?

Somewhere along the way however, a breakdown in communication came. The love, respect, and care for one another got lost somewhere. The nurturing, passion, love, communication and all those other factors needed to keep a marriage alive, simply was not there any longer.

What I do know is this – for me personally, it was God that brought **ME** through what I believed to be at that time, one of the most horrible, embarrassing and emotionally painful challenges ever experienced in my life. I had no choice but to totally depend upon God. If I did not – or had not – I would have physically died. It was during this life challenge phase that I asked God to heal my spirit, soul, body and heal me emotionally. To do so though, He had to strip my spirit, soul, body, and emotions. It was not a pretty experience nor sight. God truly does answer prayer, and He will help you if you sincerely want to be helped. I just did not know my own help from Him included divorce.

Before I proceed, I want my readers to clearly understand this book is about how God brought **ME** through my life challenges – not exposing or demeaning my ex-husband and father of all my children. We have forgiven each other, God has forgiven us both, and we are moving forward with our separate lives. Real love covers a multitude of sins. That covering comes by praying, fasting, forgiving, being quiet, not criticizing, or being judgmental and pointing fingers of accusations.

It was a lesson I personally learned almost too late. I did not know how not to do so, because I was not taught how not to. I learned by trial and error what it means to "say less and pray more." No one has the right nor room to be judgmental and critical of anybody else. Thank God for bringing me out of the land where regret, shoulda, coulda and woulda reside. I give Him glory and praise every day for placing me in the land of "doing it right, by doing it God's way." I further learned that no one has the right or authority to try and get toothpicks out of someone else's eyes and they have gotten tree trunk limbs sticking out of their own. Neither am I at my house looking through a periscope into someone else's closet trying to count how many bones are hidden in their closets. I've got enough in my own closet to open a new cemetery. Some things are best kept only between you, God, and the person (or persons) involved.

Now that my disclaimer is out of the way, let us move forward. During my separation and divorcement phase, I cried myself to sleep many a night. I truly could not understand what was happening, but I had sense and strength enough to understand one thing. That God was in control and I had no choice but to totally depend and lean on Him. He was the Executive Producer of this situation, and obviously had the leading role in the production. A pruning and refining process started which literally made me a piece of clay in the Master Potter's hand. What I did know without any doubt was, if I did not trust God in and for this, I would die not only spiritually but physically. Learning to yield myself to Him and the Holy Spirit's leadings, eventually unfolded reasons beyond my wildest imaginations as to why this divorce had to occur.

Before the unfolding though, I begged God to please let me have any test but this test. I forgot it's the teacher who determines the type, when, what, and where tests are needed and given for their students, not vice versa. I really wanted God to save the marriage. It was hard for me to even bear the thought of divorcing. Not only did I cry endlessly, but I also hurt badly, felt embarrassed, humiliated, and like the laughingstock and "hot topic" of church. I did not know at the time; I would have to cry and emotionally die to truly live.

Neither did I know then that God HAD to be my top priority – even over and above marriage or the lack of one. I had been so busy focusing, crying, and lamenting about my then husband's actions, I had lost sight of God's purpose for me whether I was married or not. Not only that, but I also did not realize I was hurting emotionally, and blamed myself for us not being married.

This separation and divorce Mid-Life phase transitioned me from a caterpillar wiggling in hot ashes, to hiding in the nook of a spiritual tree limb. I did not know God was the one who put me in the nook of the tree limb. He had to hide and protect me because He had to perform emergency spiritual metamorphic surgery. Now, I cried even more tears because I knew I was about to be isolated and transformed. My old self-righteous, woe is me nature was about to be peeled off like onion skin, wrapped up in spiritual plastic wrap like a cocoon, my spiritual chest cavity sliced open and my heart circumcised.

Lord knows I did not volunteer nor sign up for this phase. I knew it would be very painful spiritually, emotionally, and perhaps even physically. Surgery of any kind makes us uncomfortable. It is unpleasant, requires recovery either short or long, and sometimes requires a period of total isolation. I was entering a valley of darkness, with no signs of seeing a hill, let alone a whole mountaintop. More frightening for me at that time was the fact I had to go through this life phase totally alone. The old nature and woman had to be spiritually broken into a zillion pieces and be completely rebuilt in God.

In the natural, my marriage world crumbled before my eyes. I submerged like a submarine into depression, emotional death and felt like a walking corpse. I could not fathom what I was going to do alone and with three children. How was I going to be able to do it without a mate and father for my children? I felt helpless because I knew it could not be done on my own. Those I knew would if they could, were trying to maintain their own marriages and homes together.

I was literally traumatized, in denial, couldn't believe and did not want to receive it. Although the signs of the impending separation and divorce kept slapping me in the face, I simply refused to accept it until the fact TKO'd me.

The emotional pain and trauma was horrible and unbearable. I thought I would snap and lose my mind. I kept thinking – what kind of testimony is this? Could I survive all this embarrassment and humiliation resulting from it? How could I face my children, family, friends, neighbors, and church family? I felt not only deeply hurt but betrayed and emotionally abused. I cried non-stop because I felt no one cared, took his side, felt it was all my fault and held me responsible.

Did God work a super-duper miracle, wave a spiritual wand, or reconcile us back together like I thought He was going to do? Nope! That was the other thing that blew me away. I just knew He would! During the marriage, God had performed a lot of creative miracles for other couples. I felt if He raised Jesus and other couple's marriages from the dead, then surely, He would resurrect our dead marriage situation. As I plowed through this testing phase, I continued to cry. The crying started ceasing when I finally understood God would have restored it – if it was His will! So, obviously it was not meant to be restored. Therefore, I had to put my big girl undies on and deal with that harsh reality.

I did not want to deal with it because it was still too painful. I loved being married. I took my vows seriously and divorce was never an option because it was never a thought in my mind. I thought I would always be married to him.

The other harsh reality of separation and divorce is this. Those we expect to rally around and support us, will avoid us. Many so called "good buddies" started rumors that the breakup was my fault. I seemed to face opposition from every side I faced. Neither had I encountered so many "sanctuary and parking lot prophets" and folks who "had a Word from the Lord" for me, in my life! People I did not even know started telling me "the Lord showed you me in a dream…" and "God's gonna send that man running back to you!"

Yeah, right! I was being bombarded from all sides, even at the grocery stores. It got to be so bad, whenever I saw someone looking like they were heading my way, I turned around and went in the other direction. They were not just speaking from their own hearts, but trying to retrieve information about the situation, so they could spread more gossip and lies. I was hurting and emotionally bleeding. I did not need misinformed, propha-lying, gossipy, rumor spreading spirits anywhere near me – especially right then.

Their opinions were unsolicited and unappreciated. The favorite line was "Honey, if I was you…." I would cut their kneecaps off mid-sentence by saying: "But, you're NOT me, are you? There's absolutely no way for you to understand or know what I am going through. You're still sleeping in the bed with your husband every night, aren't you?" Oh, and please let me not forget the know-it-all single women who have never been married, trying to put their two cents in. "Girl, I would poison him. He would not know what hit him." "Pack your bags and leave because you deserve better." God showed up and out even in my emotional pain and made me spiritually astute enough, so I could get away from them.

An Oasis In My Valley of Baca

If I had not been rooted and grounded in the little things of God as I was, all the negativity and non-support could have physically killed me. The gossip, rumors, false accusations, lies, judgment, criticism, and isolation were already killing me emotionally. I was truly a wounded warrior who was being finished off by her own troops. My comfort zone had changed into some very deep and unsettling waters. If I were not careful, I would drown.

I kept wondering where all the super-deep people were who could discern 30 demons in a person? I could not understand why they could discern that, but could not discern my damaged emotions, broken heart, and pain? Was not there anyone who understood or cared what was happening to me at all?

I heard people laughing and whispering as I walked past them. I heard about those couples whose marriages were already shaky, filing for divorce after they learned about our impending one. Those already shaky marriages decided if our marriage dissolved after so many years, why should they pretend everything was all right with their marriage, when it was not. On the flip side of the coin, I witnessed other couples drawing closer together. I bless God still for those who showed love and support. They cried with me, hugged me, encouraged me, built me up in the Word of God, came by and took me out, ministered in finances and food.

The good ending to those who shunned me is this. Many years later, a few of those same couples apologized to me for their behavior. They said they did not know how to respond to me and my situation. Therefore, they cried behind their own closed doors, prayed for me and the children, and loved me at a distance. I always tell people – truth has a big mouth. She tells everything. We may be dead and gone, but she will find a way to expose it. That is one reason when I minister or teach, I tell on me. I try to live my life as an open book. I am not perfect and never have claimed to be. I have done some incredibly stupid stuff I am not proud of, and which could have also been very damaging to my entire family. Oh, thank God for mercy, grace, forgiveness and covering.

When people go through separation and divorce, that is not a time for other people to ignore them. They are still the same person; they just do not have the mate we were accustomed to seeing them with. Suppose I was a widow? Would not others respond and rally around in support? Well, the problem was, they did not understand I felt like I had lost a loved one. The difference was, the other mate was still alive and walking around.

Because of various so called "saints" open, visible, and true felt actions towards me, I cried even more, and put up non-penetrating brick walls of defense. I intentionally purposed to keep myself and my children as far away from spiritual roving reports, assuming minds and know it alls. I felt very insecure and did not trust anyone anymore, except a very few. I entered an outright way and determination we would not become laughing and gazing stocks to the people we knew.

I was not thinking about hearing nor quoting scriptures. If people started quoting scriptures to me, I cussed them from Amazing Grace to How Sweet the Sound! People (church and unchurched) with good intentions told me I would look back over this negative situation, and not even remember the pain and anguish. A few even had the nerve to say God would send me someone who would make me forget all about my children's father. I did not want God to send me anyone else at that time. I wanted the man I had been married to almost 20 years.

Why couldn't anybody understand that? While all those thoughts were nice and sounded super-spiritual, I did not want (or need to) hear any of it! I am sure they meant well;

however, the emotional pain then was so deep, I did not think I would ever recover.

In reality, I did not want to let go emotionally. I felt there were too many years invested in the marriage to give up without a fight. I could not understand why we could not just come together and weather this storm if God were on our side. After all, did not we vow to be together "for better or for worse, richer, or poorer, in sickness and in health?" During the marriage, he willingly and patiently covered me with love and prayer when I sent him through changes. Did not he know and understand I was more than willing to do the same for him during his "Life Change Phase?"

I cried and kept bothering God to fix it! Then one day, out of the blue, the reality indicator light started flashing like an ambulance siren. It kept flashing "It takes three to make a marriage work! You, your spouse and God!" All three must agree and believe they want the union to work. The real eye-opener and most important flashing light said, both must find out if it's even God's will to be married to each other in the first place! I was facing a real life, 23 years of placing a "cart before the horse" situation! I never knew I needed to seek God first, to find out if I was supposed to be married to him. I did not know I was supposed to! More tears flowed at this reality, and I felt totally stupid!

Realistically, I did not know how to let go. I had been with this man since age 17. He was my earthly everything and world. I was not only afraid of being alone, but of the uncertain unknown. The thought of being alone, feeling rejected by people, talked about, and feeling I failed as a wife and mother, terrified me. It was years later before I was scripturally taught differently. The teachings and environment I was in at that time, made me feel that way. It was a long time before I discovered my worth and value in God's eyes and He loved me in spite of myself. Remember readers, I am letting you know where I was at *that* phase in my life.

Spiritually, way down in the pit of my belly, I knew and loved God enough that He surely had a reason for allowing separation and divorce to occur in my life. It was Him that gave me the comfort and strength to endure the emotional pain. Even in all of these emotional and rollercoaster ride experiences, I never questioned His sovereignty. What I did do was cry an awful lot and told Him I did not understand. I did ask Him, however, what I could have done to prevent the separation and divorce.

His response was it was ABSOLUTELY NOTHING I could have done to prevent it! This is a situation designed to give Him glory, honor, and praise, and it was destined to be. It was not my responsibility to understand, just obey, trust, and depend upon Him. It was at that moment, Proverbs 3:5-6 became embedded in my spirit, and still my favorite scripture today: *Trust in the Lord with all thine heart. Lean not unto your own understanding, but in all thy ways acknowledge Him, and He shall direct thy paths.* My three keys – Trust, Lean Not to my thinking, and Acknowledge Him! That is all I must do, and He will take over from there.

All that was well and good, but I was NOT prepared to feel like I was roasting on a holiday grill like a slab of ribs and chicken parts. My emotions at that time were shattered in so many pieces, they felt like the old fashioned, crushed up communion cracker sacrament. Seems like I was the selected choice for open emotional and spiritual target season. It was a fight to my very core. I was afraid I would be taken out because I felt unequipped to fight this demon. I did not know then that I already had the victory!

While sluggishly moving around feeling sorry for myself. A male minister friend called and invited me to lunch. He prefaced by reassuring me that he was not trying to 'get with me', but he had a Word from the Lord he needed to impart to me. My infamous left eyebrow raised up, but I felt the Holy Spirit prompting me to go. We had a blast, and he made sure to keep me laughing, so I would not "embarrass the family by breaking out in tears in the public!" After lunch, he pulled out a piece of paper from his jacket.

This is the gist of what he told me. It may appear that I was losing the battle. However, God was actually working the whole situation out for **MY** good, and **His** glory – not my ex-husband's! He had no choice but to release me because he had been a hindrance to what God had ordained **ME** to do. This situation was also an all-out spiritual war that God Himself had to handle – not me. My instructions were very simple:

"Moving forward from the point of us sitting at that table, I had to do what God said do. My very life depended on me completely trusting Him, not leaning to my own understanding, seek Him for direction in every area. If He does not speak or send confirmation, then I was not to make a move. I was to be steadfast and unmovable in praying for myself, the children, and others, and do not compromise my Godly standards for anyone, no matter how tempting it looks, or how much I am offered, etc. God was going to use this situation – and future situations in my life – to set His daughter free! He has plans for me that will blow me out of the water. I had no idea how powerful and anointed I really am in Him. While I may be crying tears of sadness now, God is going to turn my tears into pure joy! He is right here with me now, and He will always be here. I will lack nothing, and within a few days, I will really know how much God truly loves me as you continue on my life's journey. In a few days, I will not even be a shell of who I am, because God is going to give me an overhaul. He has to purge me from my old way of thinking and seeing who He really is. He has to uproot all those negative seeds that have taken root in my spirit and do

*a repotting. The process will not come to me overnight, but it **will** come in **HIS** time. I will not even know when the transformation is complete, but others will start saying how radiant and glowing I am. I will look so different to some; they won't even recognize it's me until I say something. God says, 'Arise my daughter, out of your place of desolation and despair, and behold the vastness of my greatness on this earth that you have yet to see!'"*

The anointing was so strong on that man, I could hardly look at him. He was glowing, and it felt like I was sitting in the presence of an angel. It was so real, I had to brace myself so I would not slide to the floor. I knew God was truly using my brother to impart life into my spirit and soul on that day. The first thing that did it was when he stated the exact same scripture (Proverbs 3:5-6) God had put all down in my spirit. I hugged and thanked him for obeying the leading of the Lord. His parting words were to be prepared because it would SEEM like the situation was getting worse instead of better. I just had to hold on and not look at situations in the natural.

My minister friend did not lie! It took all of my energy to get out of bed every morning. I still just could not believe I was going through this. I still continued to cry. I was still angry, bitter, paranoid, defensive, hard-hearted, and very insensitive to anybody else's needs. The focus was on my pain, instead of Jesus the pain reliever. I knew I would eventually wake up from the horrible nightmare, soon, or just wake up in the face of God Himself in glory.

Despite all these strange occurrences, and I still cried all the time, something inside just would not let me give up on God, nor hate Him. Some days I felt like I wanted to just die, because I thought I did not have a reason to live anymore. While I was not thinking about committing suicide, I just felt like I wanted to go to sleep and wake up in heaven away from the earthly madness.

An Oasis In My Valley of Baca

My world of an ideal marriage and family had crumbled to dust before my eyes. I could not stay focused or motivated and it took all my strength to get out of bed, get the children off to school and get myself to work. Thank God for those prayer warriors who stood in the gap for me, because God knows I could not pray for myself. I was headed into a very deep valley of depression.

God gave me the grace and strength to feed my children and get them off to school. As I reflected over that time, I do not know how I managed to humanly function at all. It was very difficult for me to face people – from neighbors, co-workers, and church members. Life had dealt me a very harsh blow, and all of the emotional wind was knocked clean out of me.

I acted like I was okay and put on a good front in public. Those who knew me well, however, knew I was not okay emotionally. My soul felt empty, the sparkle in my eyes had faded, my joy was completely gone, and my spirit was very deeply wounded. I felt – and looked – like I had aged 20 years overnight, and shoulders drooped in heaviness and dejection. It was difficult for me to look people directly in their eyes, hold my head up, or hold a decent conversation without breaking down crying in mid-sentence.

In God's timing and overnight, the healing process began. I heard a pastor ministering on the radio that lit a spark of hope. He was explaining who we are in Christ, and it did not matter what we were going through – separation and divorce after being married almost 25 years; just lost your job, etc.! He gave scriptures about who God says we are in Him. Old things were passed away, and behold ALL things become new! This got me real excited and gave me a determination to get up and stop moping.

I had spent four months in seclusion, wallowing in self-pity, and even stopped going to church. I decided to go

An Oasis In My Valley of Baca

visit Mother Perry. Baby, she let me have it and snapped on me like a turtle. She put one hand on her hip, pointed her finger in my face and said something that shook me all the way back to reality.

"Look-a-here now, Chaaa-maine! Enough is enough You gotta make up in yo' own mind 'bout this thang! You can continue moping 'round here looking silly as a Christmas goose if you wanna. You can also decide if you gonna live again. You can get up, brush yourself off, stretch out on God and start living! I'm tired of you walking 'round here looking like a rag-a-muffin and ya' hair all matted up like a Brillo Pad! You ain't old and you far from being an ugly woman. They're plenty good Christian men out here looking for a good, well-kept, intelligent, Christian woman like you. Still got a whole good life ahead of you, Chile! That husband is gone on with his life without you, and he ain't thinking 'bout you. I suggest you do likewise and choose to live, cause I ain't tryna bury you, and I'm too old to be tryna raise your churins!"

I felt like Sophia when she came out of her rocking back and forth half-crazy state at the dinner table! That last sentence hit me, and I started laughing until my sides hurt. Only this time, I was crying tears of joy and release. I knew the cloud of sorrow and despair had been lifted. You would have had to know Mother Perry and envision her saying that. She was known for her dry wit and humor, not cracking a smile, and putting her right foot up and down while reading you the riot act. She had very big eyes, and wore Coca-Cola bottle glasses, that magnified her already huge eyes! I think seeing her do that is what did it.

After I went home, the hidden scriptures of affirmations regarding who I was started stirring my inner being. I got down on my knees and asked God and the Holy Spirit to help me get through this situation. I released everything to them — my emotions, my hurt, my heart, and my thoughts.

An Oasis In My Valley of Baca

I said out loud if they wanted me to stand and believe for the restoration of the marriage, I was willing. If they wanted me to release the marriage and no longer fight, then they would have to show and give me the strength to do so. I knew I could not handle it or do it alone.

My answer? I was told to release the marriage *and* the man and let it all go. I had done all I could possibly do humanly. When I consented to do that, I felt a small feeling of release, but it still felt like I had a huge knot in my chest. I got up off my knees, picked up my Bible and it fell open on Psalms 118:17 – *You shall not die, but live and declare the works of the Lord.* (KJV) When I turned the pages of the Bible again, it fell on the passage of scripture in Ephesians 6:13b and 14a – *...having done all to stand, stand therefore.* (KJV)

As if that were not enough to make me Queen of the At-Home Carpet Ministry, the Bible opened to Isaiah 54:4-6 *Do not fear, for you will not be ashamed; Neither be disgraced, for you will not be put to shame; For you will forget the shame of your youth, And will not remember the reproach of your widowhood anymore. For your Maker is your husband, The Lord of hosts is His name; And your Redeemer is the Holy One of Israel; He is called the God of the whole earth. For the Lord has called you Like a woman forsaken and grieved in spirit, Like a youthful wife when you were refused, Says your God.* I do not think it can get any plainer and directly to the point than that!

These three passages of scripture began the next phase of my healing process. They also miraculously aroused my spirit from its comatose state. I had a race to finish, and I was not quite out of this game called Life just yet. I jumped up from the spiritual boxing ring floor and began punching the demonic forces as hard as I could with God's Word and prayer, until I gave them all TKO's! It was time for me to ride the sails with Ms. M.'s life winds of change. I chose to live and not die! I was also astute enough to know I may be out of the barn stall, but I needed a little more grooming and exercise before heading to the starting gate.

This phase of hiding was one to start my inner healing process. I cried a mixture of sorrow and tears of joy this time. Sorrow because, this had to be done by hiding myself in the nook of the life phase tree! Joy because nobody will even recognize nor remember my cocoon phase, including me!

CHAPTER 7

A Well of Oasis in the Valley

Mother Perry's words ignited the fuse that got me motivated and start living again. In the natural, my recover process seemed long and tedious. I learned to take one day and one moment at a time. Spiritually, I knew I was right on course with God's divine destiny for my life. I still woke many nights in cold sweats, and my pillows wet with tears a lot. However, I was determined to survive. My children needed me, God needed me, I needed myself and all of them.

Of course, it was still a challenge, and neither was the struggle over by a long shot. I had to work through a lot of emotions and feelings. I was indeed healing from the battle war, but a great way yet from re-entering the battlefront lines. I literally had to learn what it really meant to look through the "eyes of faith" and not give in to what I saw and felt in the natural.

After the marital separation, I rarely went anywhere. I had no desire to go to church at all, and I did not. One thing I am not, is phony and pretentious. Everything was not okay, and I did not have the emotional stamina to deal with nonsense or answer questions that was nobody's business. Neither did I want to cuss people out in the sanctuary, nor the church mothers rushing me down to the altar for deliverance. I wanted to just be left alone so I could heal emotionally. I was in a very dark place. I felt if I stayed away, then they would stay away, and guess what? They did! That let me know they did not mean me any good. None of them ever bothered to call, send a card, or drop by just to see if I was still breathing or not.

My outside activities during that time was limited to work, taking the children out for recreation, going to the mall with close friends and a movie. It was difficult to venture out alone, mainly because it caused me a lot of emotional pain to see other couples hugged up and all lovey-dovey. If anyone has any inkling of Satan's tactics, then you know that he had couples placed everywhere I turned. It was like he was constantly reminding me that I did not have anyone to be all lovey-dovey with, and it hurt bad! In other words, I was messed up from the floor up emotionally! It felt like I had open heart surgery without anesthesia. Ironically, deep inside I also had the strong conviction that if I could just hold on a while longer, I knew I would come out victorious.

A while after Mother Perry's great cold-water-in-my-face wake up revelation, another male friend (now deceased) invited me to lunch. He became a very dear friend and confidant and was the one who God used to help pull me out of my many emotional ruts. God supernaturally used him to help me understand I was not unattractive, and that quite a few men had been asking about me. They wanted him to talk to me and set dates up with them. I fell out on that one. Someone thought I was fine and wanted to be seen in public with me? Did they not know I had gained almost 70 pounds after my separation and they still wanted to be with me? They wanted to know why no one had snatched me up as a wife yet, because a lot of men thought I was a treasure, and all I needed was the right man to make me sparkle. I was really shocked at that statement!

An Oasis In My Valley of Baca

Why would anyone want to marry me, and what did they see attractive about me? I felt like a throw away, and useless towel. It was hard for me to believe any man could find me attractive enough to want to date me, let alone marry me! Me – beautiful? Chile, Puhh-leeze! My self-worth was so low during that time, I felt ugly and nobody would ever want to be with me again. The only reason I went to lunch with my friend was because I knew I would be safe because he was from the LGBTQIA community and like a big brother to me. He always came by the house to check on us and make sure we had food to eat.

He also gave me my second cold-water-in-the-face wake up slap. He rebuked me hard for not acting like the royalty he knew I was. He said it was my classiness, beauty and tact that attracted me to him as a friend and sister in the first place. He had overheard me cracking on a married deacon who was trying to hit on me and take me on a date. He said I sent the man running for cover like a roach when lights are turned on. I could not remember the incident until my friend told me what I did.

He said my left eyebrow shot straight up, I walked over to the church microphone, hit the unmute button, and publicly thanked him including his wife (who was nowhere around) for calling me at 10:45pm the night before informing me he had hotel reservations at a swank hotel, inviting me to have dinner at one of the exclusive restaurants inside the hotel, then join him in his top floor penthouse suite. My friend said he started waving his hands for me to be quiet, and they almost had to carry him out on a stretcher. My friend said I was acting like I was dusting off the organ near the mike and said all of that into the microphone while acting totally sweet and innocent. One of the church mothers came up and started beating the crap out of the deacon with her purse. She told him to leave me alone, pushed him to the altar, started praying and telling that whorish spirit to come out of him. The pastor came out of his office, after hearing all the commotion, told the deacon and church mother to go wait in his office. The pastor apologized for the deacon's nasty behavior, and he would be 'sat down' from the deaconship office.

He also applauded the way I conducted myself and the creative way I handled the situation. I started laughing when my friend told me about it, but I remembered very well. I heard the man's wife finally divorced him on the grounds of adultery. He continued trying to seduce every new female that visited the church.

My friend said I always carried myself in a Godly, classy manner and did not act like other women. We also worked together in corporate, so he saw me in both elements. I did not act one way on Sunday, and like the world the other six days. When he heard me check the deacon, he said his assessments proved to be correct. He knew I was serious about my walk with the Lord, and my marriage. He also knew I was not trying to be at every social event, nor trying to sleep my way into a high paying position, but I was always encouraging others and giving them appropriate scriptures. He esteemed and respected me so much, he even told our co-workers to stop inviting me to the after-work, let it all hang out gatherings. Because of my commitment to God, he also became more serious with God, and eventually stopped hanging out with them as well.

Our friendship blossomed, and he became the closest thing to a biological brother I ever had. He also gave me a good dose of my own medicine, by scolding me for thinking so little of myself. He said I was so full of wisdom, anointed and knew my scriptures so tough, that my very presence intimidated people. He could not understand why I could not see and know how much God loved me and was concerned about me? It was he who started me on the path of realizing I was royalty and a joint heir with Jesus Christ. I was not less than, I was not junk, and I was not a peon. Then, he made me almost spit my soda out when he told me if I were not cute, he would never be seen in public with me because he did not want anyone contaminating *his* good looks!

He charged me from that day forward: "Never forget I was God's daughter and a joint heir with Jesus Christ! I have a royal heritage and to never think of myself as being useless or worthless again!" I often think his divine mission was to be in my life during that time, because after he helped get me together emotionally, I moved to the west coast, and he died unexpectedly about six months later.

Do not get it twisted, I still struggle with my value and worth, especially when I see other drop-dead gorgeous women in passing. They have body shapes some women can only dream of, and are vivid reminders of the time when I was a size five, memories of which are just a vapor. The flip side of that is, no one knows but those women how they really feel about themselves emotionally. We can only see the outward beauty, and do not know their hidden emotional pains. I learned to be content in whatever phase, size or shape I am in. The most important thing is, I am still on top of the earth and not under it, and I am sane enough to know I am still here, I can walk, talk, hear, and see without trouble. In other words – I am blessed!

One day, I was really feeling down emotionally and physically. I went to the grocery store. Did not bother to fix myself up or anything. Put on a jogging suit, slicked my hair back and left the house. It seemed everywhere I turned; I saw all these beautiful women. I had gained at least 75 pounds since the divorce and felt huge – and I was. I felt ugly, and afraid I would run into high school classmates who always teased me about being so skinny. If they saw me now, they would not even recognize me. Then, I saw what the enemy was trying to do. I shut him down by starting to thank God out loud for being alive and healthy right there in the grocery isle. That tormenting demon lifted off me, and I was all right.

When I "came to myself" I heard a woman's voice saying: "Baby, stop staring at the lady so hard. It's not nice to stare at people like that!" As I approached them, I saw the cutest, brown eyed little boy about four years old. He was staring at me like I was a favorite toy. He reached over and touched my hand. At first, I thought he and his mother overheard me thanking God in the isle. The little boy looked up at his mom and said: "But Mommy, I like her cuz she soooo pretty!"

I was overcome with emotion and started crying right there. Then his mother said: "Yes, Baby – she is *very* pretty, but it's not nice to stare at people!" I gave that little boy the biggest hug and kiss and told his mother she had no idea what her son's remark had just done for me. Then she hugged me and told me everything was going to be all right, and she would be praying for me.

To some readers, it may seem the above is trivial or unnecessary. However, for me, it was God's way of letting me know, in a very special way, that He can use a child, in a public place, with witnesses, to affirm my worth to Him, and we cannot outdo His outpouring of His great love for us!

After driving myself back home amid the tears of joy, I went to the bathroom, inhaled deeply, looked in the mirror and did a visual self-analysis. 1) My nose did not spread over half my face; 2) Hair needed to be done, but I had a head full of it; 3) Skin was not covered with acne or warts; and 4) Yes, I had gained a whole lot of weight, but with eating modification and exercise, losing it was not impossible.

I took another step towards recovery and repeating what God's Word said. Psalm 139:14 (*I will praise thee, for I am fearfully and wonderfully made*), became my sustaining self-worth and value to God scripture. I repeated it every time I could until I saw a miraculous outward manifestation. My outward countenance and appearance visibly changed, and within a matter of days, my skin color turned noticeably lighter.

These daily, all day long affirmations helped me not only recognize, but continue to operate and walk in my kingdom position as God's daughter. My life – and yours – depends on knowing who we are in and what our positions are in God. These discoveries helped me keep my head lifted high. Not because I think I am all that, a bag of chips, a coke, and a smile. It's because I KNOW who I am and whose I am, and I plan to stay free and flow in this vein until Jesus returns!

The cocoon shell had slightly cracked, and a new person was starting to emerge. I finally felt emotionally strong enough to be around people again. I started fixing myself up, bought a couple of new outfits, etc. It had been a long time since I felt this good about myself and where life had me. I really did not think I would arrive at this point ever again.

The other thing I did was to make sure to only surround myself with positive, spirit-filled people. They were the ones who stuck by me and protected the little emotions I had left. I was still very emotionally fragile, though. I was also determined to continue protecting myself, and they made sure it happened.

As I continued the fight to regain my sanity and dignity, interesting things began to develop. Every scripture I turned to give me the same confirmation in some form – "God was with me, He loved me with an everlasting love, He was with me in every situation, trust in Him, lean not to my own understanding, acknowledge Him in all my ways, and He shall direct my paths!"

One day I realized, I was not crying at the drop of a hat anymore. I could talk about my ex-husband without needing to take anti-depressants. Gradually, it became easier for me to function on a daily and consistent basis. The emotional pain was slowly dissipating from around my heart, my will, and my emotions. I emerged inch by inch out of despair. I was being led towards God's light of real love at the end of my emotional tunnel.

I sensed the Holy Spirit's presence in my room during the stillness of the night. Encouragement nuggets came through the radio or TV at those points I felt I could not stand anymore, and about to give up. Every time I started to waiver emotionally, God hit my life rewind button and put me back to a right frame of mind.

Amid the emotional moments of the enemy trying to remind me of what happened, the Holy Spirit comforted me and gave me inner peace. I still had good and bad days, but the good days soon started outweighing the bad. The full outward manifestation still was not there yet, but I knew something good was happening inwardly. After about four months of "forsaking the assembling together of ourselves" (that is, not going to church), I finally felt strong enough emotionally to do so. I knew it was time to get back in the sheepfold of spiritual protection and move on with my life. No more moping around feeling sorry for myself and missing out on God's purpose for my life. It was now up to me to break out of Dr. Deadly's clutches and be free. An emotional jailbreak to freedom had to be done. I chose to live instead of plummeting headlong into an emotional spiritual AND physical death.

When I walked through the church doors, people greeted me in tears and excitement. Many people told me they had been praying for me to get through the nightmare. Some cried and asked me to forgive them for not calling or coming by to see me. They expressed they did not do it because they were so hurt and devastated about the situation, they did not know what to say or do. Others stated they did not contact me because they were afraid, they would say the wrong thing and send me into further depression and emotional pain. I cried with them, because God had given me the answers, I sought Him about feeling forsaken and alone. To other people, the fact that I walked through the church doors, was an open answer to their secret prayers.

The loving and forgiving actions of the church members confirmed again that God really love me and cared about me. I had learned to seek and rely on Him for my very existence – and I still do, to this day. If He does not direct and lead me, I do not or will not do anything. One of the reasons is, I was so distraught emotionally during that time, I was very afraid I would mess up, regress, and have a mental breakdown.

God also proved in the smallest ways how concerned He was about the children and me. Every need was met, and even some of my desires for an ice cream cone. To some readers, that may not seem like much, but it was a supernatural fulfillment for me. The weather was scorching, and I had no extra money for a single ice cream cone. I had just finished expressing to the Lord how I would sure love to have a couple scoops of ice cream. It was not even a good ten minutes later that one of my girlfriends came by unexpectedly to take me for a ride, just to get out the house.

She took me right to the ice cream parlor, then to the mall to window shop. I am surprised my neighbors did not call 911, I cried and praised God like I had lost my mind. It was all because God had heard my seemingly insignificant desire for scoops of ice cream on a hot summer day. What a mighty God I serve!

I sense you rejoicing and praising God with me for this testimony, but it was just the first of many victories and surprises from Him. I was snatched from the clutches of depression, a nervous breakdown, emotional and physical death. I need you to hold steady right there and put your Pentecostal dance shoes up. The fun part had just begun.

I had a strong urgency to move out of state, after the ice cream incident. I felt I was getting back into life's flow and restructuring my life. At first, I thought my imagination had shifted into overdrive. I did not know anyone in California except my favorite Uncle and his son. All my close family and friends lived in the city I was born and raised in.

Soon after my relocation urges, three guesses and the first two do not count – guess who called and asked me to consider moving to California and handle the administrative aspect of their business? I felt like the Virgin Mary who asked the angel "How could these things be?" As God so divinely orchestrates things, my job at that time scheduled me for a business trip to California. Coincidence? No, it was not. While there, I felt like I had been there all my life. The feeling was so strong, it scared me, and I kept getting confirmations.

When I returned home from that trip, everything in my comfort zone suddenly turned topsy-turvy. My once open doors were unexplainably sealed tighter than a cemetery burial vault. Even more weird was, everything that was changing, was in direct correlation to the time my Uncle needed me to come there. Did God have me mixed up with Abraham or something? How could I *"get thee into a far country away from my kindred?"* Unlike Abraham, I was NOT rich in cattle and land. I had no visible means to trade anything for cash. I did not even have enough money to go on a backyard camping trip, let alone leave the state. It was all I could do to try to keep my children fed and clothed. I also knew, however, if I had missed God, I could always repent and come home to Mother Perry.

I wanted to know what God was doing to me now, what was really going on, and why was there such a sense of urgency to leave the state right then. Did I miss God on this one? How could I leave when I had just become separated and about to be legally divorced in a few months? The separation and upcoming divorce wounds were still very fresh and sore, and I was still hurting and healing emotionally.

In the natural I resisted because I was scared, but my gut was screaming I had to make this move. It was so strong, I knew if I did not do this move, I could physically die. I kept receiving confirmation after confirmation to move. I still did not pack my bags and take the next thing smoking out of town. I did the same thing most people would have probably done. I kept saying that God would not tell me to do this because I have children I need to finish raising, and they need me. God would not tell me to up and leave everything and everybody, especially at a time like this! I kept saying that surely God would not let me be a laughing and gazing stock, and be put in another position of a hot gossip topic.

What would everybody think if I just upped and left, especially if I left the children? Could not their father use that as a leveraging tool and say I deserted them and gain full custody of them. Even if I wanted to take the children with me, they had just started school and my oldest daughter was entering her senior year of high school. I envisioned everyone screaming and carrying poster signs saying, "Child Deserter!" Here comes the return of the river of tears!

God has not and will never change. He is the same today, yesterday, and forever more. He causes upsets and stirs up the winds of change. He can and will hurl us out of our comfort zones and thrust us into the unknown in the twinkling of an eye. No matter how unsettling it may appear to be or feel, He is doing it to fulfill His divine will and purposes for our lives. Scripture has shown us repeatedly how He leads His people to unfamiliar territory, and even painful paths. That very thing we are bucking against, and not obeying God in, is oftentimes the very thing God is using to protect us from sudden destruction.

The icing on this relocation phase cake was this. My estranged husband came by unexpectedly one day. I explained to him about my Uncle's offer, my concerns, and my fears. As a matter of fact, it was the most free-flowing, heart-felt communication we had, had since the separation. He did not hesitate to agree to move back home and take care of the children. They could stay in school until after Christmas break, move to California in January and enroll in school. He added rest assured we know that WE both made this decision together. It did not matter what anyone on the outside thought, felt or wanted to believe. If God knew, we knew, the children knew, and our parents knew, it was not anyone else's business.

We prayed, hugged and he left. I cried mixed tears this time. Tears of joy, unbelief, and fear. His understanding and willingness to cooperate, move back home and take care of the children, knocked me totally out of the water. We really had not spoken or talked to each other since he left. I knew then, God was at work in the spiritual realm on my behalf. I also knew He had His hands all up in this phase of my life. I just did not know exactly what, though.

Just as we predicted, when word got out that I was moving out of state, the gossip mill went into play. Many assumed it was because I was so shaken by the marital dissolution, I was running away. Much prayer, supplication and faith enabled me to stay focused. I did what I felt God was telling me to do, no matter how it looked to other people. Spectators and nose-zeeka-leekas were all up in our family's lemonade pitcher with no sugar to sweeten, nor a spoon to stir.

I was still being transformed from the inside out, and the metamorphosis was still painful to the point of tears. God was hardening the slime of life in the hole and breaking up my fallow ground of emotions. I did not know I was in for some up and coming very big surprises and rude awakening, that was still yet all part of my transformation process. God ushered me out of my comfort zone inside the tree nook, right onto the potter's wheel. He prepped me for emergency surgery, strapped me on a spiritual gurney, and pushed me into the spiritual operating room for divine destiny reconstructive surgery.

I cried again because I knew God was the one doing this necessary surgery. He is the great physician and Chief Surgeon of Precision. He specializes in removing whatever malady has invaded our spirit, soul, mind, will and even our emotions. He would make sure I did not emotionally nor physically die but live and declare His works!

Lastly, I cried during this emergency spiritual surgery phase because I saw a light of hope at the end of this life phase tunnel, and this time it was not a freight train of death and destruction!

An Oasis In My Valley of Baca

CHAPTER 8

Out of Baca Valley, But Still Thirsty

As we continue our life's journeys, we all find out that things never work out the way we think they should. Neither do the fairytale visions "living happily ever after" ever manifest. No one is perfect, and no situation is perfect. There is always that thing in life called "reality"! My situation was no different. The new waters gave me a crash course and huge pitchers full of it.

I was awarded the "Ms. Naïve Queen" more times than I care to discuss. I had lived a pretty sheltered life growing up as a child, and a virgin to the world's methods of operations. I had no "street smarts" so to speak due to my middle-class lifestyle upbringing. As such, I was clueless as to how treacherous (traitorous, disloyal, faithless, deceptive, backstabbing, two-faced, double-dealing, cheating, false, dangerous, crooked, and unsafe) the streets can be. Momma and Daddy Perry, along with Granny Grady, made sure I only learned about the finer things of life. Thank you, Sweet Jesus!

My world as I knew it growing up, consisted only of home, school, church, piano lessons, traveling with family to various functions and different states with people of these same types of social class. Any youth group outings were also very well chaperoned by trusted adults, so even that kept me sheltered. If we thought about doing anything ungodly, those chaperones would appear out of nowhere and be on us like bees swarming a honeycomb.

There was a completely different breed of people in this new place. These ways included (but were not limited to) moral standards, thought patterns, basic common sense, and just life in general. It was a dog-eat-dog world. I witnessed for myself, people doing any and everything, just to get what they wanted, and climb their success ladder. I saw (and was even a victim of) undermining, blatant lying, two-facedness, removing and placing of important documents from files, people pretending to be friends just to get information and use it against them, falsifying and doctoring documents, and a lot other open ungodliness. Everything I was taught to value and deem precious in life, seemingly had no existence there.

My top-notched and highly sought-after administrative skills meant nothing there. It was a land of who you knew and what you were willing to do to not only get it, but keep it – not what you knew. If I had not had the fear of God embedded so deep in the core of my being, I could have very easily jumped right on that wagon. Those Godly principles played a major factor in my not yielding to the offers and carrot dangles presented to me. More surprising, disgusting, and unbelievable was, how many so-called men (and to my surprise) women were perpetrators of the gospel.

I cried because I faced a series of disappointments and made quite a few wrong choices. However, even in my disappointments and wrong decision makings, I never doubted that I was still in God's perfect will and plan for my life. I knew the life winds of change had driven me to this new and unfamiliar phase. It was my divine mandate to stick it out and let God help me work it out, no matter what!

An Oasis In My Valley of Baca

My first disappointing 'out of the tunnel' life blow was the day I actually received the officially stamped divorce papers. I had been separated, relocated to another state, adjusting to my being 'single' status, and finally starting to move on with my life going on two years now. I *thought* I was prepared to receive the final divorce papers. However, quite the opposite was true. Receipt of those papers snatched the scab off my emotional wound that I thought had been totally healed. The reality and truth of finality was a big, bitter pill to swallow. The papers in my hand made me break down and cry. Holding them was a painful reminder the emotional hurt of being separated and divorced was still lurking in my heart. Those papers were also a harsh reality check that I was no longer loved by the one who once claimed they loved me.

More tears flowed as further realization came that perhaps he never loved me in the first place. That thought was enough to send someone who slept beside a person over 19 years, carried and bore their children right into a psych ward. It was also the day I understood that emotional attachments and soul-ties just do not go away with the wave of a Bible and quoting the scriptures in them. It takes time for God to heal emotional wounds and scars, and HE is the only one who can do it. We just must understand this – that it's in His time, not ours!

God had already instructed me to release the marriage. I really thought I had done so. In all honesty, in the recesses of my unrealistic state, I kept believing we would only be separated for a season, and then reconcile. I felt this phase would pass, and he would return to me and the children. In my ignorance and stupidity, I even envisioned us on national television, telling the world how God had miraculously restored our marriage! How nutty is that? We cannot make anybody – male nor female – be with us who does not want to be with us – especially if they point blank tell you to your face they do not!

I knew I did not initiate the divorce and never wanted it. Neither was it so much that it happened, it was the *way* it happened that almost sent me over the edge. If I had not developed a solid relationship with God over the years, I would be in eternity with Him. My heart would not have been able to physically stand it otherwise. Holding those divorce papers in my hand on that day assured me it was God's will for me to be divorced.

Those papers made it very clear that we cannot over-ride another human being's will or make our will their will. People are going to do what they want to do, despite of us. That includes as mentioned above, making them love us. As powerful as God, Jesus and the Holy Spirit are, even they do not force themselves on us, nor make us love them. Time for another big dose of my 'reality meds'. It was a very bitter dose, but if I wanted to live, I had no choice but to gulp and swallow my Valley of Baca drink all the way down!

Disappointing reality awakening number two was due to unforeseen circumstances (which I later understood was God's divine intervention – again!). The job with my Uncle never fully got off the ground. It felt like I was about to be blown away by the winds and storms of life again. My children were with me by now. I made the foolish mistake of trying to wait for the house they grew up in to sell, instead of working until it sold. I did not know any better. Neither did I have wise Godly counsel to inform me how the selling and homebuying process really worked. It was not until after the fact that everyone came out the woodwork offering advice. I did not know selling property was time consuming and detailed. I believed once property was placed on the market, it would be sold within a couple of weeks. Although I did not have a clue what to expect then, I can surely tell you how not to make the same mistake!

An Oasis In My Valley of Baca

I was not only embarrassed, but too proud to call home and ask for help. I did not want anyone to know I had messed up and did not have a job. I moved out of state to make things better for me and the children – not worse. In my stupidity and self-righteousness mind, I felt it was 'beneath me' to find work, even if it meant working in a fast-food restaurant, just to make sure my children were well provided for. In my ignorance, would you believe God *still* showed me mercy and kept me from total ruin. I still cry in thanksgiving when I remember those select few people who readily helped us out during this time and will always be grateful to God and them.

I was reluctant to seek help because of the way I had seen "super saints" helped other people. It was nothing nice. Their ways of helping was to announce who they helped, how they helped, and how much they dished out monetarily to help. God supernaturally provided a way of escape and gave me a wonderful job, with great benefits, and it helped bring me up and out within a few months.

Shortly after working, my third reality awakening occurred. I had to silently endure malicious lies and character assassination because I refused to submit to the "wiles of the devil." Another jewel was obtained in my Ms. Naïve Queen of the Century crown when I learned there are *"Devils in the Pulpit!"* I thought I was in another Twilight Zone sequel with this encounter. God came through and prevailed again on my behalf. It took a little time, but the truth came out in my favor in the end.

This experience taught me to be on guard for ravening wolves in sheep clothing. Jesus even spoke about them in the New Testament. They are ministers all right, but they are really Satan's ministers of darkness. They look, smell, and even act like ministers, but are sent to abort God's divine purposes for God's people. It is written, however, that Satan and all his cohorts ends is destruction and hell fire.

During my "still not out of the woods yet" life phase, I got betrayed and used by a few ministers. Many were angry with me because I would not join their church, allow them to make me their spiritual puppet, or become their "church side-chick." This one particular minister maliciously lied on me because I refused to sleep with him. He could not persuade me in any manner to 'win me over'! When he found out I could not be bought in any manner, that is when he tried to destroy me with his lies. He spread lies around that he not only paid all my bills off but put me and my children in our own home. He told people I showed up at his house, opened my coat and did not have anything on underneath my coat, asking him to pay bills in return for oral sex. I really hollered at that lie, because at that time I was wearing a size 22 and was not about to show ANYBODY what that looked like naked!

Secondly, how could I show up at his house, and I did not even know where he lived? He got good and exposed when he was in a meeting of ministers and tried to tell them that same lie about me. Two of the ministers stopped him mid-sentence and busted him stone-cold out! One said, "She must be a magician and can make herself be in two places at the same time. We do not know how she could have possibly been at your house at the time you're saying she was. She and her assistant were at a meeting with us and our wives at the time you claimed she showed up at your door flashing! You might want to be careful about spreading those lies on that Woman of God!"

The other minister added: "Man, everybody knows you're a womanizer and male hoe! You probably showed up at HER house flashing!" Oopsy! Busted! I did not hear from him anymore up close, nor did he try to approach me ever again. If I were in a public setting and he saw me, he would get a frightening look on his face, and immediately go right back out the door. I laughed because he did not have a reason to be afraid of me. I had not done anything to him. Who knows, maybe he had a visitation of the Godkind that scared the baa-jeebies out of him. This time I cried because God had openly avenged me from this man's vicious lies.

An Oasis In My Valley of Baca

CHAPTER 9

Fresh Rain in the Baca Valley

This chapter deals with my most rewarding life phase experience. As mentioned, I eventually got a temporary long-term assignment, which ended up turning into a permanent full-time position. However, because I did not operate in Godly wisdom, the children and I almost became members of the homeless population. God intervened again, and we ended up living in a transitional living home my cousins operated. Again, God did not forsake us, and we were not begging bread. It was in this 'low' place that my fourth dose of reality hit me hard. Remember, I told you of my middle-class upbringing. Well, my cousin's transitional housing consisted of recovering addicts, alcoholics, prostitutes, functional mental patients, murderers, and former drug dealers!

I wanted to be whole, but I was not prepared to be spiritually bone-stripped and shattered into zillion pieces. God is the potter, and I was the clay in His hands at that moment. Most of us are not willing to let the Potter shatter our clay pots of humanness. Why? Because the cracking and remolding process is nothing pleasant. Yet, God does it for our own best interests and well-being.

Ironically, as only God can do, it was in that transitional living phase that I grew even closer to God. It was also when God dissected me and revealed a lot of hidden things about myself, many of which was not very nice or pretty. I had a lot of emotional and spiritual residue that still needed flushing out. There were even hidden hurts and wounds going all the way back to childhood molestation by family members – male and female.

However, the worst shock was when the Holy Spirit showed me that I was arrogant, self-righteous, judgmental of others and very ungrateful, and a spoiled brat! I fell on my face in repentance with a quickness.

I realized I took a lot of things for granted. I was spoiled in the natural and always thought people owed me something. It still humbles me and makes me cry when I remember how horrible I was before God came in and changed me inwardly.

While on that subject, if our paths crossed and I offended you (knowingly or unknowingly), either by my conduct, self-righteous attitude, in my conversation, you felt my walk and talk did not line up, please forgive me. I am so Godly sorry. I made a list of people I knew I had offended, repented, and asked God to forgive me for hurting them. I also repented for any shame and embarrassment I did to anyone in the Body of Christ.

I even forgave those who swore I had wronged and offended them, when in fact the opposite was true. They deliberately lied on me, tried to sabotage me, and did everything they could to destroy my character, integrity, and credibility. There were a few God removed from me and said He would deal with them Himself! I sure would not want to be in their shoes! I got word that one person was trying to find me and beg my forgiveness. Seems ever since he was paid to "plant seeds of doubt regarding my holiness walk and bring me down off my spiritual high horse, he had been robbed, beaten, and left for dead in an alley!" Neither could he get a good job anymore because someone was "paid to plant an illegal substance in his government job desk!" He also lost his family, house, and car, and is now in a wheelchair. It all started after he spread all these lies on me.

He said his life had been a living nightmare, and if they ever saw me to please forgive him, pray and ask God to remove the "curse" that had come upon him for messing over me. Wow! Another God vindicating me victory!

All this unraveling of myself was so overwhelming, I could not stop crying! I did not know I was that horrible. God also revealed things in my marriage I should and should not have done. These revelations in no way indicated the marriage would not have still ended, only that some things that occurred might have had different outcomes. I even called my ex-husband and asked him to forgive me for all the negative things and grief I had unknowingly caused him, or that he felt I had done wrong in the marriage.

Listen, Sweetcakes! I was not about to let anything stand in the way of my relationship with God with a root of bitterness trying to spring up in me. I did not want my fellowship with God broken on my part. He has been way too good to me!

God's revelation made me become very grateful, appreciative, and humble. I hurried up and got off my social, sophisticated high horse. I developed compassion and a new love for all people, regardless of their social status, or race.

I grew up in a lower-middle-class environment, and never wanted for anything. I did not get everything I wanted but had everything I needed. As such, the Spirit of Pride had been ruling and reigning a very long time. Thank God for His illuminating floodlight showing me I did not! I found out later, so I purposed to do better.

An Oasis In My Valley of Baca

Growing up and in my teens, if a person did not look or act a certain way, attend MY church, or shopped where I shopped, I had low or no tolerance for them. If I did not always have at least $5 in my possession, I felt broke. That was a whole lot of money back then – comparable to having $100 today. I had the audacity to look down on others if they did not have the level or quality of things I had.

Even worse, I found homeless people disgusting! How ironic is that since I ended up being almost on the brink of that myself! I quickly changed even that after seeing a skit where everyone kept ignoring and/or mistreating a homeless man. The bottom line was, two teens hugged him, shared their food with him, gave him a scarf, gloves, hat and put money in the homeless man's pocket, and shared the love of Jesus with him. The 'homeless man' stood up and started removing his raggedy clothes and revealed that he was an angel sent to seek true-hearted believers.

There was so much crying and repenting after that skit, it was unreal. I have never forgotten it, and it made me have a completely different attitude towards the less fortunate. I had the nerve to think I was doing God a service when I gave a man or woman begging on the street a dollar. It was not really a bad thing; except I would usually have anywhere from $75 – $200 in my purse on my way shopping for 'stuff' I really did not need. Neither did I allow them to get close enough to touch me, because I felt they were too dirty, and they stank. I was afraid they would mess up my designer suits!

You think that is bad? How about me getting up in church testifying how I gave to the less fortunate? What a farce! I am glad God did not snatch my breath clean out of me for that mess. The outward appearance of me being kind and loving was there outwardly, but my heart and spirit were desperately wicked! I still cry to this day about how foolish I was during that time. I did not know what it meant to have

An Oasis In My Valley of Baca

God's heart of love and compassion for people. All I knew was to do things for an outward show.

God fixed all my erroneous mind set good. He knocked me off my high and haughty attitude horse in this situation. No one could have made me believe I would ever be a paycheck away from being homeless myself one day. Life has a real great way of turning around and biting you in the butt so hard, your butt will have teeth impressions in it. I was the top candidate to receive the holier-than-thou-self-righteous-grand elite-modern day Pharisee of the century award. All I needed were gold tassels and bells ringing around the hem of my golden garment!

I was so messed up; I just knew I really had it going one because I was at church almost every time the doors opened. I was involved in almost every choir and auxiliary imaginable in my church. God showed me that was the problem! I was *churchin!* I did not know anything about developing a relationship with Jesus, and to make Him Lord of my life. I did not even know I needed to. I was saved, in church and serving on church auxiliaries. That was all I thought I needed to do and be.

I really did not know any better at that time. It still takes all my faculties not to run to an altar and repent all over again when I remembered those days. Thank God for the precious blood of Jesus and His forgiving power! My life was one of religion, tradition, and emotionalism. I had the inspiration and motivation, but the correct information nor revelation about the things of God. I did not know I was supposed to lead people to Jesus and not the church. I did not know that Jesus was about establishing His kingdom in the earth realm, not necessarily in a church building.

All those years I was thinking I was a strong 200-Watt light bulb, showing others the way, and I was a disconnected utility current line in their way! They could not see Jesus because I was in their way! It was revealed I was not even a stove pilot light. My 'power' was not even connected to the main power line, and I did not even know it! God was not getting one ounce of glory in my Pharisaical behavior and wasted a whole lot of years' operating in the flesh. Praise God for revealing so I could repent.

I saved the best part of this chapter for last. It was by far the best and most beneficial life phase experience for me. Why? It's because it was in this transitional home where God truly nurtured and grew me up spiritually. In His own time, He delivered me miraculously and supernaturally! This deliverance disappointed a lot of people because they all expected me to fall AND fail. A few even prayed I would go back to Illinois because they were not getting attention and accolades anymore from me!

The transitional living situation taught me many valuable lessons. At first, I cried a lot because I felt embarrassed and humiliated about living there. If someone came to visit me from out of town, where would they stay? In the transitional house with what society labels rejects? They would not look at the fact my cousins owned it, and I had become the Resident Mother and spiritual advisor. Those I knew, would take just the information of me living in a transitional housing and make it headline news!

At first, I did not perceive the transitional house as a ministry nor a job. I saw it only as a temporary housing with a bunch of social rejects. I kept asking myself did I really leave a fully furnished home I had lived in for over 15 years to end up in a place like this? My answer to myself was "Hell, Naw!" My thought processes began to shift gears when God started showing me that even there, His hand was heavily upon me and the children. We were not on the street homeless and hungry. We had a roof over our heads, decent clothes to wear, three meals a day, and I had a job.

An Oasis In My Valley of Baca

The more I started interacting with the residents, the more compassionate my heart and spirit became. Most of them were from good Christian homes and affluent backgrounds. It was these same residents who I first perceived as social rejects that taught me a lot about myself. I truly was not all that!

The residents taught me not to be so quick to judge and label a person on how they looked, dressed, acted, or even smelled. Some residents shared how their life situations occurred and they just could not cope, so they did what they knew to do at that time. They did not have the Word of God to sustain them, so they chose the most comfortable and easiest escape route. A couple of them had gone through very nasty divorces that sent them to alcoholism, substance abuse and even prostitution. Thank you, Sweet Jesus, because it could have been me confessing instead of listening. God's hand was even on my children because God protected them as well. The residents could have influenced them so negatively, they could have easily been led to drug addiction, prostitution, theft and God-forbid, destitute!

The life lessons in this transitional home also showed me how we can have everything this morning, and absolutely nothing this afternoon. It was living there where God literally stripped me to the bone emotionally and spiritually. All my interest and focus on material things quickly vanished, and soon forgot about all the material comforts I had left behind. Later for designer clothes and latest fashions, too! I was in a different place, but the difference was, this time I had a peace that far surpassed my understanding. The most important thing to me was making sure my children and I were safe and working towards getting our own dwelling.

As God continued to demonstrate His favor, the more tears of joy I shed. Although I was in an uncomfortable and adverse circumstance, I never stopped reading, praying, attending church, and encouraging others as much as I could. It was very rewarding to share about God's goodness despite our circumstances, and to see rays of hope on the other residents' faces.

Another life lesson learned while there is, it's imperative to let somebody know if you're hurting emotionally. Tell the truth so you can get the help you need to pull you through. Sometimes, as you start talking about it with someone, the answer comes to you as you talk about it.

Here comes the good part! Ironically, this transitional living experience re-lit my dormant teaching fuse. The more I explained and taught God's Word and His unconditional love to the residents, the more they wanted to know about Him and the Christian walk. Many of the residents came to understand it was not God or their family who took them from their life of affluence, wealth and security to mental issues, alcoholism, substance abuse, and perversion, but demonic influences.

Some wholesome relationships developed from sharing the positive things of God. The more I taught and displayed unconditional love to them, the more they wanted to know. They began to trust me, open and shared some real horror stories. Oooo-whee, Chile! Some things confided to me, make the Mass Murderer Milton, Teddy Twinkle-Toes, Thieving Twilley, Hard Hat Harriet, La'Transvetee, and Madame Brothel look like hosts of heavenly angels. I learned to keep a straight face, not faint in shock, not criticize, or judge the things they confided about to me. It was not only because it was the right and Godly thing to do, but it is also because other people's lives were at stake to the point whole families could be taken out. They had to feel safe enough with me to be able to bear their souls and know they would not be betrayed. If there was a situation where I felt someone in higher authority needed to be notified, I had let them know for their own protection.

An Oasis In My Valley of Baca

In most cases, I had to look like I knew what they were talking about. I do not mind telling you readers that I had to hit these rusty knees on many days and ask God for His wisdom in counseling them. I was so naïve when it came to being street smart, it was hilarious. I did not know diddly about the "struggle to come off the street hookin'; going through drug withdrawals or trying to go straight after being in a long homosexual relationship"! I praise the Lord for not ever encountering any of that, BUT Satan had me bound in more subtle ways that were not so obvious to me, but to everyone else. Hallelujah for God delivering me from those 'secret sins' after showing them to me. I will tell you in a heartbeat how messed up I was, and how He broke up MY fallow ground.

The only thing I knew to do regarding the residents 'taking them to the graveyard with my secrets' was to give them God's Word, show them where they needed to repent, ask God to forgive them, go and sin no more. One thing I learned about unchurched people is this – they do NOT like pretentious and phony people or hypocrites. These are the people you must be real with. They love, appreciate and respect when you are point blank and do not sugarcoat! What I ministered to them was always in line with God's Word. What was always so amazing to me was when the Holy Spirit would give me the exact scripture they needed!

Another exciting revelation was when God revealed those residents are the exact type of people He goes after. These are they who have lost hope, are depressed, oppressed, abused and ready to throw in the towel. With a flick of His finger, God turns hopeless situations around and sets people free, spiritually, emotionally, physically, and financially. They never, ever go back to those places again, either!

It got to a place, I started anticipating one of them knocking on my door in the midnight hour to get their own special "Word from the Lord." A few of them were not quite strong enough (or did not know how to) go to the Word for themselves, so they had to be spoon-fed for a while. I laughed when various residents would give me high five slaps, or secret nods the next day. These were the ones who thought they were the only ones coming for one-on-one counseling in the 'midnight hour'. God had this thing so divinely orchestrated, that none of them ever ran into each other when they came for counseling or ministry.

God also supernaturally enabled me to immediately wake up alert and minister with His anointing and wisdom. It was as if I had been pumped full of vitamins. I was never tired or sleepy the next day, either. God had me on a roll, especially when I had to get up and go to work the next morning. The more He allowed me to expound His Word to the residents, the more revelations manifested to me for them. Their hunger pushed me to dig deeper into God's Word for myself, which made it possible to have a right then, on-time word for whatever their situation needed.

Teaching and sharing the Word of God became a vital part of me. I could (and still can) teach and minister under the anointing for hours on end and never get tired. It seemed a new compassion and love had developed for people that I could not explain. I readily embraced the reeking, unwashed alcoholic without passing out from their body stench. They were God's creations just like me. We all need encouragement and emotional build-up sometimes. Besides, it's much easier to tell people about soap, deodorant, and mouthwash *after* they're fed and built up their worth and value to society.

I rejoiced with them when they made it through the day without taking a hit or declined a roach and blunt. Of course, they had to explain to the Naïve Queen that did not mean they would hit anybody, put a bunch of roaches in a bag and tried to smoke them, and a blunt was not being mispronounced as a baseball 'bunt' hit!

An Oasis In My Valley of Baca

If a resident slipped off their sobriety or abstinence wagon, they were always encouraged to try again. I often reminded them I was in no position to judge anyone because *"All have sinned and come short of the glory of God"* and that included me!

I realized God was doing some kind of great work in me. Sure, I had taught His Word before, but it was never this fulfilling. A feeling of euphoria came on me every time I ministered, either there or publicly. I became restless if I could not teach or minister. You see readers, Satan had me so messed up. He had me believing I was unworthy to do anything for God. How could I possibly tell someone what God could do when my own marriage had failed, and here I was living in my cousin's transitional house. How could I help someone else recover, when I was in an emotional crisis's recovery mode myself?

The Holy Spirit showed me one day that ALL of God's children are recoverees! All of us have been recovered from the clutches of Satan's grip. We also have testimonies about being a recoveree of something Satan had every one of us bound up. It's in sharing our deliverance and recovery that we continue to remain free and give others hope for the same. Others will also see how God uses our life's mess ups and turn them into messages of victory. A true recoveree readily admits they will always be in recovery status until they cross over into eternity. It is no different with the children of God. Our flesh dies daily, along with any sins that separate us from God. We should be seeing angel wings, halos, and harps if the so-called saints have it all together. We do not see those things because nobody has it all together! The only place for that is in glory, Sweetcakes!

I learned life's circumstances have no bearing whatsoever on God's calling on and purpose for your life. If you're called – you're called. If you're blessed to be called AND chosen, that is even better! The Bible gives plenty of examples where God used ordinary people with imperfections. I was no exception to this rule. God used my phase of life 'upset' for His glory. Who would have ever thought God would use me to minister salvation, hope and deliverance in a transitional home filled with what the world calls 'social rejects'? I became living proof if there is a calling on your life, God will use you wherever you are, whether it's the pit or the palace! All He wants is a willing and available vessel!

As you have probably figured out by now, it was in this transitional home that my "calling and election was made sure." By the time I got my own place, I knew down in my sanctified soul that regardless of my circumstances, I was still called, chosen, and ordained to be a teacher and kingdom builder for the glory of God.

Those secret sessions with the residents helped me understand how God can take whatever you have, wherever you are, and use you. If He used a big fish, a jackass, rooster, and rock to fulfill His divine purposes, He can surely use you and me.

The residents taught me some very valuable life lessons as well. They taught me how to chill out, relax and enjoy life. I had a really bad Martha the Busy Bee spirit in full operation. I felt I had to always be doing something. I did not know how to just sit down and be still. I could not stand seeing dust on furniture, papers strewn all over the place, clothes on the floor, floors needing vacuuming, etc. I am still trying to pinpoint where I got that crazy "everything has to be in place" spirit from!

One day, I was all over the place cleaning and polishing. Two of the male residents snatched the broom from my hands, picked me up, sat me down in the living room chair and told me not to move. Of course, I protested! They gave me the TV remote and told me to watch TV. They came back a few minutes later with a plate full of dinner. It was so good, too! Next thing I knew, they were waking me up to go get in the bed. I had been asleep four hours! That was my beginning point of taking time to physically rest.

The residents taught me on that day I was not indispensable, and I could be physically replaced. They did everything I usually did, and much better than I did, too! They shattered my false illusion that the world would not stop if I were not around anymore. The reality is this: We not only can be replaced, but we WILL also be replaced! Sometimes the replacement occurs even before the person being replaced has been embalmed good! This reality made me cry again.

People who do not take time to rest and relax have died prematurely from stress, cancer, heart attacks, strokes, diabetes, and other maladies simply because they never took time away from the hustle and bustle. They thought the world revolved around them so much and could not do without them. They had the "but people need me" disease so bad, they even called their job every five minutes when they were supposed to be vacationing on an island. The main purpose of a vacation is to get away from the daily hustle and bustle of work and life, enjoy God's beauty and be still! When I was working, people like this thought I was nuts because I used ALL my vacation time.

God Himself rested on the seventh day! If He took a day to rest, what is wrong with you? We are NOT super-saints, nor are we God. Therefore, hang up you Super-Saint cape, red leotards with matching red boots, and your Super Wonder Belt! God is the only entity that can be in more than one place at one time, and be everything to everybody – not you, Sweetcakes!

God had filled the empty void in my life spiritually, emotionally, and physically. I learned in this place that it was not about being married or single. It's about obeying God, being complete in Him, and knowing your worth in Him. Although I was married many years before divorcing, there was always this nagging feeling of unsettling emptiness. Oh, the tears of joy that flowed when I knew only God fills every void, in every hidden nook and cranny, He did in the way that only HE can!

An Oasis In My Valley of Baca

CHAPTER 10

Out of Valley Detox and Moving Forward to Rehab

So far readers, you have read some situations I encountered and endured emotionally, spiritually, and physically. Through every situation, God was still merciful and blessed me despite of my messy situations and mindset. All three children graduated from high school and two continued to college. My oldest daughter successfully entered, and still is in, the music entertainment industry as a song writer and back-up singer.

However, it seemed every time I would get it together in one area, I was being strapped back on the potter's wheel and broken to pieces again. Eventually, it finally hit home that a lifetime of breaking will always be necessary to our healing and wholeness process. This chapter is designed to offer simple statements with scriptural principles to back statements up. Both genders can apply them when facing life challenge encounters, as well.

I admonish all readers to first seek God for yourself. Most of the time He uses others like me to confirm what He has already told you. The following admonitions are general statements, but sometimes we all need to get them all the way down inside our spirits. We are crying and having spiritual intestinal pain because we need a good, spiritual colonic. We have cried over issues for years which have caused parasitic and poisonous growths down in our inward parts.

I received most of these life spiritual applications as I faced my own life challenges and issues. It was not until I came out of them that I understood that I had to go through every single challenge and issue for God's glory – not mine! It was also to share these 'normal life' experiences with others to assure they are not alone, nor unique.

The key to being able to finally stop crying, not give up and die is about CHOICES! I explained earlier that God does not force Himself or His will on anybody. It's up to us to decide what we want and need to break the chains of bondage and be totally free. There are a lot of other things God delivered me from, as well as situations; He made ways of escape for me. If at least one reader is helped in any way from these key principles I applied to my own life, then my mission has been completed.

These principles should not only bless you, but help you realize God has set this appointed time for you to receive the information and to bless your spirit, soul, mind, heart, and emotions! Time to dry those tears and understand God has not forgotten about you. He loved you enough to not let you die, regardless of what you have gone through. God chose you the reader to make it, if nothing else but to read this book for encouragement and hope!

1. You MUST put God first in EVERYTHING, and I mean EVERYTHING! This includes seeking Him as to whether you should even leave your house or not. It's not only a safety measure for you, but it also relieves undue burdens and prevents unwise and ungodly counsel.

Remember, if you belong to God, you have an ever-present enemy lurking to kill, steal and destroy. *But seek first the kingdom of God and His righteousness, and all these things shall be added to you.* (Matthew 6:33 - NKJV).

2. Give God His due FIRST! I am not going to get into a tithing debate. Do as you're led in your spirit, and do not allow anyone to brow-beat you, make you feel guilty, nor coerced into giving your last money. I will just say this – do you think God will honor or bless you less if you paid your house note instead of "going down and putting money in the preacher's hand"? Exactly! *Honor the Lord with your wealth, and with the best part of everything you produce.* (Proverbs 3:9) *and Give, and you will receive. Your gift will return to you in full pressed down, shaken together to make room for more, running over, and poured into your lap. The amount you give will determine the amount you get back Give, and it will be given to you.* (Luke 6:38) [Paraphrasing]

3. Do not EVER put a person, place, or thing in God's place. It's our duty to love Him with all our heart, mind, and soul. *Thou shalt have NO other gods before ME.* (Exodus 20:3 - KJV)

4. Openly and unashamedly acknowledge God alone as your source for EVERYTHING. He puts people and opportunities in our pathways, but always remember that He is the source that makes it happen. *I will lift up my eyes to the hills from whence comes my help? MY help comes from the Lord, who made heaven and earth.* (Psalm 121:1-2 - NKJV).

5. Always remember aging is a very normal process. It's not normal to look and act the same way you were 20 years ago. Accept and embrace life's body, mind, and emotional changes. It is all right with God to face the harsh reality that we were not born to stay young forever or until Jesus splits the sky open. Wrinkles and age lines will come; your hair

will turn gray or silver; your joints will sometimes ache; some – if not all – of your teeth will have to be filled, capped, or replaced. You will eventually get to a point where you forgot where you put the dishrag, and your eyesight may get dimmer than what it once was.

The good news is, we *can* look as if we are 30 instead of the age 50. Our youth can be renewed like eagles. The secret really is not a secret at all. Outward manifestations are God's rewards to us as we age because we are in a right relationship with Him. It does not matter if you're female or male. No Mid-Lifer should be acting like fickle teeny-boppers, pimp daddy's, or menopausal hootchee mamas. That type of behavior brings no glory to God at all, and it displeases Him. *When I was a child, I spoke and thought and reasoned as a child. But when I grew up, I put away childish things. Now we see things imperfectly, like puzzling reflections in a mirror, but then we will see everything with perfect clarity. All that I know now is partial and incomplete, but then I will know everything completely, just as God now knows me completely.* (1 Corinthians 13:11-12) [Paraphrasing]

6. Remember that life is a continual growth process. Therefore, continually perfect and establish yourself, spiritually, intellectually, emotionally, and even physically. *The Lord will perfect that which concerns me…;* (Psalm 138:8 - NKJV)

7. Make a quality decision to find, get in and stay in your own rightful place in God, and let Him lead you to the RIGHT pastor to shepherd you. They must first and foremost be Shepherds after God's own heart. *And I will give you pastors according to mine heart, which shall feed you with knowledge and understanding.* (Jeremiah 3:15 - KJV)

8. Live only up to GOD's expectations, not man's! *For I know the thoughts that I think toward you, saith the Lord,*

thoughts of peace, and not of evil, to give you an expected end. (Jeremiah 29:11 - KJV)

9. Be who and what GOD created you to be, not what someone thinks you should be. *Wherefore the rather, brethren, give diligence to make your calling and election sure: for if ye do these things, ye shall never fall:* (II Peter 1:10 - KJV)

10. Release ALL unforgiveness, bitterness and any grudges of the past. Unforgiveness is a great damper on and hinders our spiritual growth and maturity. If you do not forgive others, God will not forgive you. *Take heed to yourselves. If your brother sins against you, rebuke him; and if he repents, forgive him. And if he sins against you seven times in a day, and seven times in a day return to you, saying, 'I repent,' you shall forgive him.* (Luke 17:3-4 - NKJV)

11. Make an all-out effort to avoid toxic and negative people. They will manipulate you and have you serving in positions God did not ordain you to be in, nor called you to. Just because a person knows how to change a tire and replace oil in a car, does not mean they are called and ordained to be a mechanic. Allowing oneself to be put in positions not ordained by God makes you an open target for not only spiritual destruction, but physical death! *Behold, to obey is better than sacrifice, and to hearken, than the fat of rams.* (1 Samuel 15:22(b) - KJV).

12. Seek God only about His plans and purposes for your life. Then, ask Him to put you on the right path to meet and connect with the RIGHT people to fulfill His divine purpose. Continue to thank Him throughout the day for favor, increase, divine appointments, and Kingdom connections. *And Jabez called on the God of Israel saying, "Oh, that You would bless me indeed, and enlarge my territory, that Your hand would be with me, and that You would keep me from*

evil, that I may not cause pain!" So God granted him what he requested. (I Chronicles 4:10 - NKJV)

13. Give thanks for your blessings instead of complaining about what you do not have.... *for I have learned to be content whatever the circumstances.* (Philippians 4:11(b) - NIV)

14. Ask the Holy Spirit for wisdom to operate in every area of your life. If you're unclear how a situation needs to be handled, ask Him. *If any of you lacks wisdom, you should ask God, who gives generously to all without finding fault, and it will be given to you.* (James 1:5 - NIV)

15. Understand that it's okay to express your feelings. If you do not, you're setting yourself up for an emotional explosion or mental breakdown. Ask God to show you the right Godly, spirit-filled, seasoned woman or man of God to go to. I do not care how saved they say they are! *Where there is no counsel, the people fall; But in the multitude of counselors there is safety.* (Proverbs 11:14 - NKJV). **WORD OF CAUTION: If you are married, DO NOT seek counsel from a single person who has never been married!** What can a "never been married person" tell you about marriage, what and what not to do? Right! Absolutely nothing!

16. Keep your confidants to a bare minimum because everyone does not have your best interest at heart. There are always hidden agendas, jealousy, envy and even those working witchcraft to block the plans and purposes of God for your life. Instead, take your issues and challenges to God in prayer. *Deceit is in the heart of them that imagine evil: but to counsellors of peace is joy.* (Proverbs 12:20 - KJV)

17. Totally release all unforgiveness, hurt and bitterness. If you do not forgive others, God will not forgive you! *And whenever you stand praying, if you have ANYTHING AGAINST ANYONE, forgive him that your Father in heaven*

may also forgive you your trespasses. But, if you do not forgive, neither will your Father in heaven forgive YOUR trespasses. (Mark 11:25-26 - NKJV). (*Emphasis added.*)

18. Take care of your body! Our bodies are designed to give us signals and warnings when something is amiss. Otherwise, we could be attending your funeral or memorial service. Ignoring those signals can and will result in severe complications that could have been avoided if you heeded the signals at their onset. Luke was a physician who traveled with Jesus and the disciples. Jesus not only did not have a problem with doctors, but they must have been necessary, even during that time. *Those who are healthy have no need for a physician, but [only] those who are sick.* (Matthew 9:12(b) - AMP)

19. Stop worrying and carrying burdens that are not yours. Jesus is the only one who saves! Pray for people, provide Godly counsel under the unction of the Holy Spirit, and practical life experiences. It's unwise to try and over-ride another person's will, and/or belittle them just because they do not agree with you. Go to bed and stay out of grown folk's business, especially if they did not ask you to be in it. *Therefore humble yourselves under the mighty hand of God [set aside self-righteous pride], so that He may exalt you [to a place of honor in His service] at the appropriate time, casting all your cares [all your anxieties, all your worries, and all your concerns, once and for all] on Him, for He cares about you [with deepest affection, and watches over you very carefully].* (1 Peter 5:6-7 - AMP)

20. Pursue your passion with a passion. Passion is that thing that burns so deep within you, that you are not happy and do not feel fulfilled unless you're doing it. You love doing it so badly, not only can you do it 24-7 non-stop, but you also do not think twice about doing it even if you do not get paid for it. All you need to do is just step out in faith and do it. *But without faith, it is impossible to please Him (God),*

for he (or she) who comes to God must first believe that He is! (Hebrews 11:6) [Paraphrasing]

21. Do not ever give up on your dreams and promises from God. Learn to wait and be patient until the full manifestation comes. Some of our dreams may not become our realities until way down our roads of life. But since God is a promise keeper, they WILL come. We just have to be patient! *For the vision is yet for an appointed time, but at the end it shall speak, and not lie: though it tarry, wait for it; because it will surely come, it will not tarry.* (Habakkuk 2:3 - KJV)

22. Tomorrow is NOT promised to any of us! Do everything you can to work on fulfilling your destiny every chance you get! *Take no thought for tomorrow, for tomorrow shall take thought of the things of itself.* (Matthew 6:34) [Paraphrasing]

23. Seek Godly wisdom to help set short and long-term goals, then visualize and confess the success of them until it manifests. For example: If your goal is to lose weight, your long-term goal would be set at 75 pounds. Your short-term goal would be to lose two to three pounds per week until you reach your long-term goal of 75 pounds. *Where there is no vision, the people perish.* (Proverbs 29:18a - KJV)

24. Learn, adopt, and put into practice immediately, the anointed word "NO"! This two-letter word, cuts through the chase, stops folks in their tracks, takes away guilt and commands a lot of respect. It's perfectly all right to tell people you cannot do or want to do something. You can end up in the hospital and cause problems in your home and health, trying to adjust your schedule and accommodate other people. Two of the best responses are, "Let me check my calendar and get back to you," and "Let me pray about it and see if this is something God wants me to do or be involved in." Remember – Every open door is NOT a

God-opened door! *But let your communication be, Yea, yea; Nay, nay: for whatsoever is more than these cometh of evil.* (Matthew 5:37 - KJV)

25. Find a quiet place somewhere, sit down, shut up and BE QUIET! Even Jesus found Himself a quiet place to get away from the hustle and bustle of life. Take some quiet time for yourself, even if it means readjusting your schedule. You will be surprised how the divine revelations flow, creative juices get stimulated, and God can finally talk to you because you're finally quiet and still. Right now, He cannot get a word in because you're so busy talking – or you're always surrounded by people and doing things for everyone else, but not taking time to do anything for yourself or hear from Him. *Stand in awe, and sin not: commune with your own heart upon your bed, and be still.* (Psalm 4:4 - KJV)

26. Only whole people can create whole relationships. Good relationships complement, encourage, and enrich each other, not tear down, and smother each other God is the only one who can fill the voids in your life, whether you're married or single. You must be a complete person yourself before trying to become involved and tangled up with another person, who is just as incomplete as you are. Only God can break every ungodly 'soul-ties'! Only He can do it because you cannot do it on your own. *Create in me a clean heart, O God; and renew a right spirit within me.* (Psalm 51:10 - KJV).

27. Laugh, live, love, and keep your own joy cup overflowing. Nobody wants to be around a Negatron, whiner, or complainer. If you do not have any joy, ask God to give you some. Joy brings not only laughter, but healing. It's only when we learn to laugh – especially at ourselves – we have then *learned* how to live. *These things I have spoken to you, that my joy might remain in you, and that your joy might be full.* (John 15:11 - KJV)

28. There is no way to win any kind of race if you never leave the starting gate and/or point. Do what you can do, know your own limitations of that which you cannot do, and do not stress out because you can or cannot do! The key is to GET STARTED DOING SOMETHING! *Therefore, since we are surrounded by such a huge crowd of witnesses to the life of faith, let us strip off every weight that slows us down, especially the sin that so easily trips us up. And let us run with endurance the race God has set before us. We do this by keeping our eyes on Jesus, the champion who initiates and perfects our faith. Because of the joy waiting him, he endured the cross, disregarding its shame. Now he is seated in the place of honor beside God's throne.* (Hebrews 12:1-2). [Paraphrasing]

29. Chill out and get out of other people and God's business. He does not need your help! The Holy Spirit's job is to lead and guide **you** into all truth, tell **you** where to go, what to do, whom and whom not to be buddy-buddy with. *Make it your goal to live a quiet life, minding your own business and working with your hands, just as we have instructed you before.* (I Thessalonians 4:11). [Paraphrasing]

30. Get in your favorite bedtime nighty-night position, pull the covers over your head and go to sleep. God already has tomorrow mapped out for you, and fretting over what may occur. Why because God already has everything orchestrated and in specific divine order for our future.... *Consider the lilies of the field, how they grow; they toil not, neither do they spin: and yet I [Jesus] say unto you, That even Solomon in all his glory was not arrayed like one of these.* (Matthew 6:28-29 - KJV)

31. Think before opening your mouth. Your words are very powerful. The spoken word can be misquoted, but it can never be retracted once it leaves your mouth. Words verbally spoken aloud will put you in situations and you will be wondering how you ever got there. It is your words that put

you there, that is how. So-called harmless talk and idle chatter have been seeds to many people's downfalls, especially when it comes to adulterous and sexual affairs. *Death and life are in the power of the tongue: and they that love it shall eat the fruit thereof.* (Proverbs 18:21 - KJV)

32. Start speaking positive things about yourself and others by being the stop sign and gossip bottle-cork! The best way to put a cork in the bone-carriers bottle is to immediately start praying for the person the bone-carrier is trying to talk to you about. I guarantee you they will think twice about coming to you as a 'Rovin' Reporter' or gossip garbage can again. *And why worry about a speck in your friend's eye, when you have a log in your own? How can you think say, 'Let me help you get rid of that speck in your eye, when you can't see past the log in your own eye? Hypocrite! First get rid of the log from your own eye; then perhaps you will see well enough to deal with the speck in your friend's eye.* (Matthew 7:3-5) [Paraphrasing]

33. Make a quality decision to not live beneath your earthly means, God-given privilege anymore. Receive in your heart and mind God's best by stop settling for seconds and leftovers. God operates in a Spirit of Excellence, and only has the best in His domain. *Beloved, I wish above all things that thou mayest prosper and be in health, even as thy soul prospereth.* (III John 2 - KJV).

34. It does not matter how many times you blow it – it's all right with God for you to get up and try again. What He does not want is for us to wallow in our mistakes and mess. Jesus was hung up for our mess ups! Be strong in the Lord and in the power of HIS might. Humanly, we all fall or make mistakes. The only one who never made any mistakes was Jesus Christ! *Have I not commanded you? Be strong and of good courage; do not be afraid, nor be dismayed, for the Lord your God is with you wherever you go.* (Joshua 1:8 - NKJV).

CHAPTER 11

God's Love Did Not Let Me Die in Baca's Valley of Tears!

With the help of Almighty God, I came out of those life challenges not only a better woman and representative of God, but healed spiritually and emotionally. The change started from the inside and worked its way to an outward manifestation. All the years of trusting God through all my pain, heartaches, and disappointments, eventually paid off after all. I learned that all things truly do work together for my good in the long run. Not only that, since I am not dead, I know there will be more life challenges as long as I have breath in my body.

I thank God every day for those who stood with me, prayed, encouraged, and taught me to persevere. I am also grateful to God for good, strong teaching and Godly support. Through these support factors, I no longer operate in fear, doubt, and intimidation. My God looked beyond my faults and saw my need. He was (and still is) there with me through it all. He loves me with an everlasting love and has all those tears I shed in His holy vial. Through the tears, He showed me and proved to me I was His very own unique creation. He dried my tears and taught me that He created me for His divine purpose and glory, and that every day on this earth is a great adventure. Through the tears and struggles, I understood I am blessed even when I do not feel like I am, in every situation. He dried my tears and kept me alive and emotionally sane, to tell others that He is a God that dries our tears, and He will not leave you! Whatever state you are in, He is right there with you.

I stated in a previous chapter that I did not always make the best or right decisions while raising my children. I did the best I could with what I knew at that time in my life. The good news is - all three of my children saw me stand amidst of many adversities. They saw me cry as I remained kind to people who we all knew were trying to destroy me. They witnessed me crying, yet not giving up, and trusting God to bring me through situations.

One of the greatest thrills right now is when my children tell me how they now understand how difficult it was for me during that time. My response is how much it was worth the sacrifices just to see them loving and serving the same God I trusted in to bring me through.

Readers, there IS hope even where you are in your life right now. Some of you may be facing at least one of the things I have mentioned somewhere in this book. To the struggling singing parents, I say "Hold On!" Your crumb crunchers will not always be in diapers. In the twinkling of an eye, they will be walking across stages receiving college degrees, working full-time, introducing you to their life mate choices, and showing ultrasound pictures of your first grandchild.

To those struggling with mid-life body changes, separation, divorce, ungodly soul-tie relationships, death of a close loved one, loneliness, and even boredom, if you want help and need deliverance, God will do it. The key is – YOU have to want it! God has not run out of anything He made. His supply is never ending and meets your needs. He is the

Creator and original designer. As such, if He does not have it, He can create it tailor-made just for you. He is a restorer and repairer of the breach. His restoration is always at least seven times more than what was taken, and He is really good about giving 100-fold returns, too!

Perhaps your children are grown, and the nest is empty OR – you're praying for them to fly away! What about my readers who have raised their children, sacrificed everything to put them through college, while neglecting your own education. Now that they're gone, take that opportunity to continue your education. You are never too old to attend school. Do not let this younger generation intimidate you. You're the one with the goods! Sure, they may have the youth and energy, but it is time for you to live. You have matured over the years and you have great wisdom. God is on your side.

For my other readers, maybe your job downsized, and you got caught in the crunch. Use that opportunity to pursue that passion you could not pursue because you were working 60 hours a week. Now you can!

This is for those who are convinced they are too ugly, too cute, too fat, and God help us all – too thin! It does not matter what size you currently are, love yourself and fix yourself up! Looking good is not limited to your size anymore. The clothing industry is finally catering to the Plus Size women and men. They have specialty stores for them just like they have had stores for the petite. God does not care if you are a size 3 or a size 43. The alternative to you wanting to be super-thin is this: You could be graveyard dead!

God does not create junk! If you're that serious about feeling you're too ugly and not pretty enough, there are plenty of affordable products on the market these days to help you look your best. You can buy hair, makeup, padded breasts and butts, foundation garments to pull in excess fat, flesh-colored stockings to cover varicose veins, acrylic nails to hide nail stubs, estheticians to remove the blackheads on your face and neck, podiatrists who specialize in bunion/callous removals, dentists to fix your teeth, and body trainers to get you tone up the flab! All of the above listed things have been created to enhance your God-given outward beauty. A lot of these services cost little and sometimes even free, especially if you're a senior, or single parent. So – what is your real excuse, now?

Isn't it funny how we always manage to find a way to do what we really want to do no matter how much it costs? Then, why not apply that same tenacity and fervor to yourself as an investment to not only bring yourself out of the slumps, but to bring honor and glory and to the one who created you in the first place? God does not get any glory when we claim to be His, and our hair is unkempt, clothes dirty and wrinkled, got on twisted stockings and mixed-matched socks, shoes running over, etc.

Do not be looking and smelling like a vagabond, instead of the royalty God designed you to be. Esther prepared her body in oils, perfume, and makeup for an entire year because she was preparing herself to go before her earthly king. She knew and was instructed that she could not go before the king looking any kind of way. Not only did she capture his heart, but he also married her, and he gave Esther her own palace for her and her staff.

I pray this book of my struggles has encouraged, blessed, and helped readers understand that life is a process, and it happens in various stages. Every challenge encountered is only a stepping-stone to God's divine purpose and will for your life. It's during these challenges that you have the choice and God-given right to choose LIFE! In choosing to cry but not die, you may notice a big drop off of so-called friends. God will supernaturally remove them from your life because they are toxic and do not have your best interests at heart.

Psalm 34:19 says: *Many are the afflictions of the righteous, but the Lord delivers him out of them all.* (KJV) My good times have far outweighed my bad times of crying and lamenting. I would not have a testimony if I had never cried gut-wrenching tears, or been tested, and you definitely would not be reading this book.

Keep living, readers! You will have the opportunity to encourage someone along these same lines. When and if it happens, pray for the Spirit of Wisdom and Counsel. Make sure to listen, do not be arrogant and self-righteous and forget 'Oh, but for the grace of God,' you could be dead and gone! There is nothing worse than a person who turns up their nose at another person's negative situation.

God allowed me to cry what seemed like rivers of tears in a valley of despair on many occasions. There were also many times I felt like a caterpillar squirming in hot ashes. But He dried my tears, made me burst through the cocoon shell, and let me emerge with spiritual wings with the strength of an eagle.

Right now, I am living in a time that has proven to be the most exciting time of my life, and it's absolutely wonderful! It's wonderful because I learned to totally depend on God and Him alone – not man! I am not naïve enough to believe I will never cry again. I already know some things will hit like a ton of bricks again before I close my eyes for the last time on this earth. Neither will I always make the right choices or be exempt from falling back into the enemy's entrapment of self-pity, discouragement, and feeling invaluable. There are times I have to read my own journal praise reports, victories, and scriptures to reaffirm my identity in God.

An Oasis In My Valley of Baca

The difference this time is, challenges may come, try to move in and host a pity party at my house. However, their name is not on my lease and/or mortgage. As such, I cancelled their party at my house, and served them illegal tenancy eviction papers!

Surely, if I did not whither up and die after my life challenges had me crying and feeling like I was going to die, then I know He will do the same for you. Spread your wings and soar to God's best in your life. Ride the wind of life changes when it comes. You are a winner!

Life will indeed make you go through a dozen tissue boxes at a time because you cannot stop crying. This book is to admonish you to hold on because God's got you. He knew you would go through this phase before the foundation of the world. Turn totally to Him. Brace yourself, get in His Word and presence. Put yourself in God's hands and completely trust Him to help you get through it. I guarantee life will make you cry. However, God's love is so vast, wonderful, and everlasting, He will let you see your oasis! Why? Because there really is an oasis somewhere waiting for you in your own **Valley of Baca!** Peace and blessings to you and yours!

Charmaine Sha'ron Perry

Biography

Affectionately called "Apostle Char" or "Elder Char," Charmaine Sha'ron Perry's passion is ministering spiritual worth and value to God's Daughters to grasp God's unconditional love, real value and worth to Him! She flows in the anointing of Teaching and the Apostolic, brings Biblically based order to the Body of Christ with God's Word and practical life applications.

Apostle/Elder Char has keen spiritual insight and astounding Godly wisdom. Her teaching ministry gifts offers audiences real pro and con life choices, humor, raw, real, and non-filtered, mixed with her own struggles and shortcoming messages. While audiences may leave her sessions holding their sides from laughter, they also leave empowered, armed and equipped to face their life's challenges.

She is officially retired and moved from Chicago, Illinois to California in December 2016 after 53 years in the secular workforce as an Executive Assistant. She is the mother of three adults – (the youngest who transitioned at age 35 in 2010), grandmother of eleven and spiritual Mom to many across the United States. Her pastor and mentor is Apostle Joy Ann Jones, Overseer of the Jubilee Praise Center Ministries in Highland, California.

Perry has another side to her, and it is business. She is the president and founder of C.S. Perry Enterprises, Inc. where she assist entrepreneurs in business and ministry.

C. S. Perry Enterprises, Inc. is a not-for-profit corporation established in 2017 that provides state-wide Professional Start-Up Services for Small Businesses, Profit and Non-Profit Corporations, Ministries, Churches, Community and Faith-Based Organizations, Administrative Consulting Services, Grant Preparedness and Life Skills Building Training.

www.ingramcontent.com/pod-product-compliance
Lightning Source LLC
Chambersburg PA
CBHW070945080526
44587CB00015B/2230